Ginat Egoz

THOUGHTS ON THE PARASHAH

BY

Rabbi Eliyahu Attias

ISBN 1-892692-44-9

Printed by Sefer Press 732-606-2589

Printed in the United States of America

Contents

Introduction

WITH DEEP GRATITUDE TO Hashem, I present this collection of insights on the weekly Parashah.

A milestone in Torah study is celebrated with a festive dinner, as the Midrash[1] learns from Shelomo HaMelech:

> In Givon, Hashem appeared to Shelomo in a dream of the night. God said to him, "Request what I should give to you."
>
> Shelomo said, "Grant Your servant an understanding heart...."
>
> God said to him, "...Behold, I have given you a wise and understanding heart...."
>
> Shelomo.... came to Jerusalem..., sacrificed burnt offerings and peace offerings, and made a banquet for all his servants.[2]

I fondly recall Simhat Torah in the Lakewood Yeshiva. By the time we finished all the day's prayers and *hakafot*, the sun had already set. Our Rosh Yeshiva, Rav Aharon Kotler *ztz"l*, urged us to eat a festive meal — not in honor of Yom Tov, since it was already after sunset, but in honor of completing the yearly cycle of the public Torah reading.

What exactly are we rejoicing over when we complete a milestone in Torah study? And how do we learn to make a festive dinner from Shelomo? His banquet was made before he had completed anything!

I suggest one answer to both questions. Shelomo HaMelech

---

1. *Kohelet Rabbah* 1:1.
2. Melachim 1 3:5–15.

rejoiced at having received wisdom with which to understand Hashem's Torah, His mitzvot, and His creation. When we complete a Talmudic tractate, we rejoice at having acquired familiarity with its principles and laws, which will enable us to learn it better next time. And on Simhat Torah, we rejoice at having acquired the background for deepening our understanding of the weekly Parashah in the coming year.

Indeed, as we go through the weekly Parashah again each year, we can and should delve deeper and deeper into it.

The story is told of a man who brought his eight-year-old grandson to the rabbi and said proudly, "This child understands Humash and Rashi as well as I do."

"It's wonderful that the child understands Torah like the grandfather," said the rabbi. "But how unfortunate that the grandfather understands Torah like the child!"

PARASHAT

Hukat

PARAH ADUMAH, THE RED COW

Zot hukat haTorah, This is the decree of the Torah....[1]

The *parah adumah*[2] is the prime example of a *hok,* a mitzvah beyond human understanding. Rashi comments that Satan and the nations of the world taunt the Jewish people, saying, "What is this mitzvah? What reason does it have?" The Torah therefore says: This is a decree from before Me; you do not have permission to question it.

The Ramban asks: Why should they pick on the *parah adumah* more than any other sacrifice?[3] He answers: Other sacrifices come to atone, express gratitude, or bring a Jew closer to Hashem, while the *parah adumah* does none of this.

But later, Rashi[4] seems to give a reason for *parah adumah,* for he cites a Midrash[5] that the *parah adumah* atones for the sin of the golden calf. "[This can be compared to] the son of a maidservant who soiled the king's palace. They say, 'Let the mother come and

---

1. Bamidbar 19:2.
2. Red cow.
3. The *parah adumah* looks like a sacrifice because it is slaughtered and burned.
4. Bamidbar 19:22.
5. From Rabbi Moshe HaDarshan.

clean her son's excrement.' Similarly, let the cow come and atone for the calf."

To reconcile this contradiction, we must first explain how the *parah adumah* atones for the golden calf.

We might explain that the underlying reason for this sin was that they relied on their own understanding to question Moshe Rabbenu. Moshe had said he would come down from Mount Sinai in forty days, and (by their mistaken calculations) he didn't come. Faced with a situation that did not fit their understanding of how things should be, they made the golden calf, which made sense to them.

The atonement for the golden calf is by doing the opposite, bringing a sacrifice that we don't understand. *Parah adumah* does not fit our understanding of how things should be, for it does not atone intrinsically. Nevertheless, we bring it and sacrifice it without understanding its reason and secret. And precisely because we bring it without asking questions, it atones for the sin of the golden calf.

Thus the *parah adumah* atones because it does not atone rationally.

In this way, the *parah adumah* is an unusual mitzvah; we do not probe its *taam* and its secret. But for other mitzvot, such as Shabbat and *tzitzit,* we certainly look for explanations.

Shabbat comes to disconnect us from worldly matters so that we will think about our mission in life.

In addition, Shabbat is a semblance of the world to come.

Every week there is one day when we will go hungry and sit in the dark unless we prepared food and light in advance. Moreover, we will have exactly what we prepared. If we prepared a pot full of meat and vegetables with seasonings, that is what we will have on Shabbat. If we prepared less, we will have less.

Similarly, in the world to come we will have nothing unless we prepared in advance. Food and light are metaphors for Torah and mitzvot, as in, "A mitzvah is a candle, and the Torah is light,"[6] and, "Wisdom... says..., 'Come, partake of my bread.'"[7] If we learn much Torah and do many mitzvot in this world, we will have Gan Eden in the world to come.

Of *tzitzit,* the Torah says, "You shall see it and remember all the mitzvot of Hashem and you shall do them."[8] This means that *tzitzit* reminds us to undertake to fulfill all mitzvot that come our way. Even before the Jews actually brought the first Pesach offering the Torah tells us that *they went and did* as Hashem commanded.... for as soon as they undertook to fulfill this mitz-vah, the Torah considered it done.[9] So too, regarding the mitzvah of *tzitzit,* when the Torah says, *remember-and-do* all the mitzvot, as soon as we remind ourselves to do the mitzvot it is considered as they were done.

Parah adumah, the decree whose reason we do not probe, teaches us an important lesson about all mitzvot: We must not make up our own reason, but only study whatever reason our Sages transmit to us.

FLEXIBLE AS A REED

This is the Torah: When a man dies in a tent....[10]

Said Resh Lakish: The Torah is a lasting acquisition only for one who kills himself for it.[11] That is, acquiring Torah knowledge takes exertion.

---

6. Mishlei 6:23.
7. Mishlei 9:1–5.
8. Bamidbar 15:39.
9. Shemot 12:28; see Rashi.
10. Bamidbar 19:14.
11. *Shabbat* 83b.

One form of exertion required is to minimize physical pleasures and material luxuries, as our Sages[12] teach: "This is the way of Torah: Eat bread with salt, drink water by measure, sleep on the ground, live a life of deprivation, and toil in the Torah."

Another form of exertion required is to fix our *midot,* as we see from the following episode involving Rabbi Elazar the son of Rabbi Shimon bar Yohai.

The Gemara[13] relates that Rabbi Elazar b'Rabbi Shimon came from his teacher's house. He rejoiced greatly and felt proud because he had learned much Torah.

He encountered a man who was extremely ugly. "Peace unto you, my teacher," said the man.

Rabbi Elazar did not return the greeting, but said, "Good-for-nothing. How ugly you are! Are all the people of your town as ugly as you?"

"I do not know," replied the man, "but go to the Craftsman Who made me and say to Him, 'How ugly is this vessel that You made!'"

Realizing that he had sinned, Rabbi Elazar dismounted from the donkey he was riding and prostrated himself before the man, saying, "I said something I shouldn't have. Forgive me!"

The man replied, "No, I shall not forgive you until you go to the Craftsman Who made me and say to Him, 'How ugly is this vessel that You made!'"

Rabbi Elazar followed the man until they reached Rabbi Elazar's city. The townspeople turned out to greet Rabbi Elazar.

"May there not be many like him in Israel!" said the man.

"Why not?" they asked.

---

12. *Avot* 6:4.
13. *Ta'anit* 20a.

He told them what happened.

"Nevertheless, forgive him," they said, "for he is a great Torah scholar."

"For your sake I will forgive him," said the man, "on condition that he never does this again."

Thereupon Rabbi Elazar went and expounded, "A man should always be flexible like a reed and not unbending like a cedar. Because of this, the reed merited being used as a quill with which Torah Scrolls, tefillin, and mezuzot are written."

Let's study this episode.

Rabbi Elazar was very happy with the Torah. He may well have been reviewing his own new Torah insights, and he felt proud in the sense that "his heart was elevated in Hashem's ways."[14]

Along came a man who wanted to chat with him. Rabbi Elazar had good reason to refuse. He saw on the man's face that he was spiritually ugly, entirely empty of any Torah content. And the Mishnah[15] teaches that conversation with such a person takes one "out of the world" — down from his level. Rabbi Elazar was justified in refusing to interrupt his learning and descend to the level of this empty person.

By way of judging him favorably, Rabbi Elazar said, "Perhaps all the people of your city are empty of Torah, and since they did not set a good example for you to follow, it is not your fault. But I am not obligated to speak with you."

The man replied, "I do not know" — I don't know who is to blame, but I do know that it isn't nice to say that a Jew looks ugly, or that he comes from a place of ugly people.

Rabbi Elazar said, "I said something I shouldn't have" — I

---

14. Divrei HaYamim 2 17:6.
15. *Avot* 3:15.

shouldn't have used the word "ugly" regarding a human being, who was made in the image of God.

The townspeople said, "Forgive him, for he is a great Torah scholar," which justifies such conduct.

Rabbi Elazar entered the *bet midrash* and expounded, "Let a person always be flexible as a reed" — for although too much conversation with an empty person is harmful for a scholar, the scholar should behave like a flexible reed, which bends temporarily and then returns to its place.

Similarly, the Gemara[16] says: If your wife is short, bend down and whisper to her.

Sometimes a man who learns Gemara in depth finds it difficult to chat with his wife. If she is not interested in speaking to him about Torah outlook, he may have to bend down and enter into simple conversation with her as an act of kindness. Rabbi Aryeh Levin recommended looking for interesting news to tell one's wife, such as who became engaged. But he should not overdo it; the reed bends temporarily and then returns to its place.

CLIMBING THE NUT TREE

He [Moshe] said to them,[17] "Hear now, O rebels! Shall we bring forth water from this rock?"

Following Miriam's death, while the children of Israel were in the desert, they had no water to drink. Hashem told Moshe to take his staff, gather the children of Israel, and go speak to a rock and it would give water. Moshe spoke harshly to the Jews and then struck the rock with his staff and it produced water.

---

16. *Bava Metzia* 59a.
17. Bamidbar 20:10.

As a result of this episode of Mei Merivah,[18] Hashem decreed that Moshe and Aaron would not bring the people into the Holy Land. What did they do to warrant such a decree?

Clearly it was Moshe who erred; Aaron was punished for not stopping him. But it is so hard to pinpoint Moshe's error that our Sages and commentators give dozens of different explanations.

One point that emerges is taught by a Midrash.

On the verse "I went down to the nut garden,"[19] the Midrash[20] explains that the Jewish people are likened to a nut. Why? Because a nut tree is smooth, and a person must be very careful when climbing it lest he fall. Similarly, whoever serves the Jewish people must be very careful lest he be punished on their account.

The Midrash proves the point with three examples.

When Eliyahu HaNavi said, "The Children of Israel have forsaken Your covenant,"[21] Hashem told him, "Anoint Elisha... as a prophet in your stead."[22]

When Yeshayahu said, "I dwell among a people of impure lips,"[23] an angel touched a burning coal to his mouth.

And when Moshe said, "Listen, please, O rebels," Hashem told him, "You will not bring this congregation to the Land."[24]

How carefully we must honor Hashem's children!

---

18. The Waters of Dissension.
19. Shir HaShirim 6:11.
20. *Yalkut Shimoni HeHadash* 117.
21. Melachim 1 19:14.
22. Melachim 1 19:16.
23. Yeshayahu 6:5.
24. Bamidbar 20:12.

ANGER

"Take the staff, and gather the congregation — you and Aaron, your brother — and speak to the rock before their eyes, and it shall give its waters...."[25]

Let's examine three of the explanations of Mei Merivah — those of Rabbenu Hananel, Rashi, and the Rambam — and find the common thread.

Rabbenu Hananel[26] explains that Moshe said, "Shall *we*", instead of "Shall *Hashem* bring forth water", a language that intimated that Moshe brought the water along with Hashem.

Rashi[27] explains that Moshe struck the rock instead of speaking to it.

Although, Hashem commanded Moshe to bring forth water from a rock at the beginning of the forty years, by striking it, here, at the end of the forty years, he was instructed to speak to it.

Says the Midrash:[28] A teacher might hit his young student in order to teach him, but an older one should be rebuked verbally. Similarly, Hashem said to Moshe, "When this rock was young you were to strike it, but now you were to speak to it.'"

Not only was the rock now older; so were the Jewish people. After studying Torah under Moshe Rabbenu for forty years, they were now on a much higher spiritual level.

Rambam[29] explains that Moshe became angry at the Jewish people and said, *Shim'u na hamorim,* "Listen, now, you rebels!"[30]

25. Bamidbar 20:8.
26. Cited by Ramban, Bamidbar 20:8.
27. Bamidbar 20:12.
28. *Yalkut Shimoni* 763.
29. *Shemoneh Perakim,* end of ch. 4; cited by Ramban, Bamidbar 20:8.
30. Bamidbar 20:10.

Says the Midrash:[31] At first, only a trickle of water dripped from the rock. Some people said, "Moshe, this is water for toddlers!" He became angry at them and struck the rock twice, bringing out water that drowned the scoffers.

In Tehilim,[32] we also find: "They provoked anger (*vayaktzifu*) at Mei Merivah, and Moshe suffered on their account."

The common thread: Anger is what caused Moshe to make the mistakes of striking the rock and of saying, "Shall *we* bring forth water."

To be sure, Moshe Rabbenu never lost his temper. He was in full control of all his *midot*.[33] *As i*t was said about the *midot* of Rabbi Simhah Zissel of Kelm; they were like a coat filled with pockets, and he took out any *midah* as needed. And when Rabbi Yisrael Salanter displayed anger to influence his listeners, he would turn aside and say to himself, "External anger, not anger of the heart." All the more so Moshe Rabbenu! Any anger of his was purely external, shown for the benefit of his listeners. In fact, his words *Shim'u na hamorim* may be rendered, "Listen, *please,* you rebels!"

If so, what was wrong?

Rambam explains that the Jewish people thought that if Moshe showed anger, it was because Hashem had told him to, for Moshe did nothing on his own. But here Hashem was not angry with them at all.

We might add that this was the *dor hamidbar*,[34] who were on a high spiritual level, especially now, after forty years in the desert. They were far removed from the sins of Korah's days. Now they

---

31. *Bamidbar Rabbah* 19:9.
32. Tehilim 106:32.
33. Character traits.
34. Generation of the desert.

believed that "Moshe is true and his Torah is true" — not only is his Torah true, but also Moshe himself is true — everything he does is from Hashem.

Yes, they complained now, "Why did you bring us up from Egypt?"[35] But their intention was: If our miraculous source of water has been taken away, evidently we are unworthy. Perhaps the next generation will be worthier.

And since their intention was good, Hashem did not become angry at them.

So the crux of the problem was that since Moshe showed anger, the people thought that Hashem was angry at them when He was not.

In any case, Moshe's sin was unintentional and for the sake of heaven. Why, then, was he punished so severely?

We may answer in light of the following Midrash.[36]

Hashem said to Moshe, "How can I let you enter the Land?" The matter may be likened to a king who entrusted his sheep with a shepherd and the sheep were stolen. The king said to the shepherd, "If I let you come before me, it looks as if I do not care about my sheep. Since the sheep are not here, you may not come."

Accordingly, Hashem had already decreed forty years earlier that Moshe would not enter the Land since his generation would not enter. But it came about through Mei Merivah to make a point: Beware of becoming angry!

Similarly, Hashem had already decreed in Avraham's time the Egyptian bondage.[37] But it came about when Yaakov showed favoritism to Yosef in order to make a point: Beware of showing favoritism to one of your children!

35. Bamidbar 20:5.
36. *Devarim Rabbah, Zot HaBerachah.*
37. See Bereshit 15:13–14.

A MESSAGE TO EDOM

Moshe sent messengers (*malachim*)... to the king of Edom: "So said your brother Israel: ...Our forefathers descended to Egypt.... We cried out to Hashem, and He heard our voice.... Let us pass through your land...."[38]

Why should the king of Edom care about the Egyptian bondage and about the prayers of the Jews?

The Midrash[39] compares this to two brothers whose grandfather had left over a debt and one of them paid it. Later the one who paid the debt needed to ask his brother for a favor. He said, "You know the debt was incumbent on both of us, but I paid it, so please do not turn down my request."

The decree of bondage for Avraham's offspring was incumbent on both brothers — Yaakov and Esav, the forebear of Edom — but it was Yaakov who descended to Egypt.

Continuing this line of thinking, we find more allusions here to Yaakov and Esav.

The messengers that Moshe sent to Edom were angels, like the messengers that Yaakov sent to Esav.

Yaakov and Esav had divided the worlds between them, with Esav taking this world and Yaakov taking the next. That is, Esav took the material world; Yaakov, who "dwelt in the tents"[40] of Torah and prayer, took the spiritual.

Esav hated Yaakov for taking the blessings of worldly abundance, which Esav regarded as his own domain. Yaakov sent messengers to explain that his interest still lay entirely in the

---

38. Bamidbar 20:14 –17.
39. *Tanhuma* 12.
40. See Bereshit 25:27; Rashi.

spiritual domain; whatever he took of this world was only for the sake of the next.

Now, too, Edom was afraid that the Jews would take away its inheritance, as Moshe recapitulates in Devarim: "Hashem said...: You are passing through the boundary of... Esav.... They will fear you.... Do not provoke them, for I shall not give you of their land... for I have given Mount Seir as an inheritance to... Esav."[41]

So Moshe told Edom's king: We have come this far only through prayer. We are still in the spiritual world, in the synagogue and the bet midrash, and we have no intention of taking your portion.

Yaakov had given Esav a costly tribute. Moshe intended to do similarly with Edom. Hashem said, "You shall buy food from them for money...."[42] — which Ramban explains: Pay them whatever price they want.

Why, then, did Edom refuse to let the Jewish people pass through their land?

Rav Zaitchik *zt"l* answered: Edom, bent as it was on material-ism, was afraid of being influenced by the sanctity of Israel, with its Clouds of Glory and its Mishkan.

LIBEL

[Moshe said to the king of the Edomites,] "Let us pass through your land. We shall not pass through field or vineyard...."[43]

Targum Yonatan explains that Moshe meant to say: We will not abduct or entice your women.

What a strange comment! Why would Moshe find it necessary to say this to Edom's king?

---

41. Devarim 2:2–5.
42. Devarim 2:6.
43. Bamidbar 20:17.

Evidently, there were Edomites who maintained that it would be good for the economy to have the Jewish nation pass through their land and buy provisions from them. But the king, in order to dissuade them, warned them that the Jews would do these terrible things.

Of course, Edom's king knew that his accusations against the Jews were false and the Jews were holy and pure. But this is the way it is, the Jews are accused of deeds that the nations of the world are guilty.

Similarly, Potiphar's wife, seeing that Yosef was holy and pure, accused him of things that she herself was guilty.

And so have the gentiles slandered Jews throughout our exile, falsely accusing us of deeds of which they were guilty.

THE LOSS OF AARON

Hashem said to Moshe and Aaron at Mount Hor by the border of the land of Edom, saying, "Aaron shall be gathered to his people...."[44]

Says Rashi: Because they had drawn close to the wicked Esav, they lost this *tzaddik*.

How had they "drawn close" to Esav?

We may point out three ways:

Firstly, the messengers had said, "So said *your brother* Israel."[45]

Secondly, some Jews had evidently gone into Edom and bought food and drink, for a good price *to please* the Edomites.

Thirdly, they *saw* Edom's abominations. Thus Moshe, in warning the Jews against idolatry, said, "We passed amidst the nations..." — and Edom was one of these nations as explained in Ibn

---

44. Bamidbar 20:23–24.
45. Bamidbar 20:14.

Ezra — "and you saw their abominations...."[46] Even seeing these abominations is liable to weaken a Jew's fear of Hashem.

To teach them not to draw close to Esav, Hashem took away Aaron, whom they all felt close to and loved dearly.

In addition, He brought Amalek, in the guise of Canaanites, to fight them. Amalek is always a whip that is ready to punish Israel as necessary, as Rashi says.[47] Previously Amalek came because the Jews were lax in Torah study; now Amalek came because they drew close to Esav.

Next, the Jews complained about the manna, evidently they had seen fruits that attracted them in the markets of Edom. From drawing close to Esav, they were drawn to material things, therefore Hashem sent deadly serpents, to teach them: Keep away from gentiles and keep away from materialism!

---

46. Devarim 29:15–16.
47. On Bamidbar 21:1.

PARASHAT

Balak

THE STRUGGLE BETWEEN GOOD AND EVIL

Balak son of Tzipor saw....[1]

Parashat Balak describes the struggle of the Side of Holiness versus the Other Side; truth versus falsehood, purity versus impurity, and the good inclination versus the evil inclination. The Torah records this entire narrative so that we will be on guard and defend ourselves against attacks by the Other Side.

The struggle has continued throughout history, with the weapons of evil changing from era to era. Today it is unfiltered Internet; in Balak's time, it was sorcery. Let's not fool ourselves. The Other Side has tremendous power, as our Parashah teaches.

The Zohar[2] points out Balak's two main characteristics: He was a master sorcerer and a master Jew-hater. He is called "son of Tzipor" because the word *tzipor* can be translated as "bird", and he would present questions to a bird and receive answers from it. And when all the other descendants of Yitro converted to Judaism, Balak did not join them, for he hated the Jews. Because of these characteristics, the Moabites appointed him their king in order to oppose the Jewish people.

---

1. Bamidbar 22:2.
2. Zohar 3:184b, 3:197a.

Balak called for reinforcements. He sent messengers to Bilaam in order to muster all the might of the Other Side against the Jewish people, using the weapons of curses, sorcery, and accusation.

Although Hashem told Bilaam not to go, he insisted on going — and Hashem let him. For Hashem sometimes allows the force of evil to rear its head, and then it has great influence in the world, supported by the superhuman power of its heavenly prince. That is why we must never underestimate the power of evil.

Thus at the Sea of Reeds, "the Children of Israel raised their eyes, and behold, Egypt was traveling after them, and they were very frightened."[3] Rashi explains: They saw the heavenly prince of Egypt traveling from heaven to help the Egyptians.

One way to fight the evil inclination in its various manifestations is found in the command regarding places of idol worship: "You shall destroy their names."[4] Says the Gemara:[5] How? By giving them derogatory nicknames.

We must fight the evil inclination by mocking anything connected with it, for this will lower its importance in people's eyes.

By mocking impurity, we nullify its power.

THREE TIMES

Balak took Bilaam... and from there he saw the extremity of the people.[6]

Balak said to him, "Go now with me to a different place... you will see its extremity...."[7]

---

3. Shemot 14:10.
4. Devarim 12:3.
5. *Avodah Zarah* 46a.
6. Bamidbar 22:41.
7. Bamidbar 23:13.

Balak said to Bilaam, "Go, now, I shall take you to a different place...." Balak took Balaam to the peak of the height that overlooks the face of the wasteland.[8]

If we know what Balak and Bilaam were trying to accomplish, we will know how to fight them today.

In their three attempts to hurt us, Balak took Bilaam to three different places. The first time, mention is made of "extremity" and "people"; the second time, only "extremity"; and the third time, neither.

The first time, they sought to arouse accusation regarding the very beginning of the Jewish people. Was not their ealiest *hinuch*[9] faulty? After all, Yaakov took the blessings from Yitzhak with deceit, and Yaakov's sons were involved in the incidents of Shimon and Levi with Shechem, Reuven and Bilhah, and the sale of Yosef.

To answer these accusations Hashem revealed the truth through Bilaam:

"How can I curse when God has not cursed?"[10] Rashi explains: Even when they were deserving of curses, they were not cursed, for upon discovering that Yaakov had taken the blessings, Yitzhak, said, "He shall remain blessed."[11] And when mentioning the deed of Shimon and Levi, Yaakov cursed only their anger.[12]

That is, their deeds were true and correct, and their sin was only a small mistake along the way. Shimon and Levi killed the men of Shechem for failing to enforce law and order; Reuven acted out of concern for his mother's honor; and the brothers sold Yosef to preserve Yaakov's family.

---

8. Bamidbar 23:27.
9. Upbringing.
10. Bamidbar 23:8.
11. Bereshit 27:33.
12. See Bereshit 49:7.

"For from its beginnings, I see it rock-like."[13] Rashi explains: I see them founded strongly by the Avot and Imahot.

That is, they received excellent *hinuch*, which they accepted and obeyed.

"Who has counted the dust of Yaakov"[14] — this refers to the dust used to cover the foreskin after it is removed through circumcision. A covenant is made between Hashem and each newborn boy, so that he grows up tied to Hashem.

"He counts the matings of Israel"[15] — their marriage is based on family purity, so that their children are born with holiness.

In summary, the Jewish people are born and bred in holiness.

The second time, Balak and Bilaam wanted to arouse accusation regarding the cycle of the year.

Bilaam wanted to say: All year long, the Jews become sullied with sins of *bitul Torah*[16] or speaking *lashon hara*.

Hashem revealed the truth:

"He looked not at iniquity in Yaakov."[17] Rashi explains: When they transgress His laws, He does not scrutinize their iniquity.

How can that be, isn't Hashem a strict, true Judge?

A clue is to be found in the appearance of this verse in *Malchuyot*[18] in the Mussaf prayer of Rosh HaShannah.

When the month of Elul comes, followed by Rosh HaShannah and Yom Kippur, the Jews think thoughts of repentance, mend their ways, and make Hashem their King.

The verse ends: "The shofar blast of the King is in him," meaning, that with broken hearts, they blow the shofar on Rosh

---

13. Bamidbar 23:9.
14. Bamidbar 23:10.
15. Bamidbar 23:10.
16. Wasting time when Torah could have been studied.
17. Bamidbar 23:21
18. Hashem's Kingship.

HaShannah. It is at this point that Hashem does not look at their sins, for they are nullified through repentance, and the Jews emerge from Yom Kippur clean as angels.

The third time, Bilaam said, "*Mah tovu ohalecha Yaakov,* How good are your tents, O Yaakov..."[19]

The Gemara[20] says that Hashem reversed Bilaam's curses and from his blessings, we know what was in his heart. What he wanted to say was that the Jews should not have shuls and study halls. The Maharsha indicates that he wanted to accuse, saying: The main thing in a Jew's life is not the shul and *bet midrash,* but his work and his family.

Hashem reversed Bilaam's accusation. A Jew begins his day by entering the shul and saying, *Mah tovu ohalecha Yaakov,* followed by, "Hashem, I love the house where You dwell...."[21] The whole day continues from that good start.

A Jew knows that the *bet midrash* is the source of fear of heaven for himself and his children, and it is there that he celebrates his son's bar mitzvah by having him called up to the Torah on Shabbat and making a Kiddush.

Having heard the accusation of the Other Side, we must muster our strength to undo it. How? By providing our children with good *hinuch,* repenting completely during the High Holy Days, and making the synagogue and *bet midrash* the center of our lives.

After attempting to curse them three times, Bilaam prophesied about Mashiah, the rise of Israel, and the downfall of the nations of the world, saying, "I see it, but not now; I look at it, but it is not near. A star has issued from Yaakov...."[22]

---

19. Bamidbar 24:6.
20. *Sanhedrin* 105b.
21. Tehilim 26:8.
22. Bamidbar 24:17.

Here Daat Zekenim, citing the Midrash, gives us the following insight:

Bilaam said that all these good tidings would take place in the distant future, but Moshe predicted they would take place soon saying, "The day of the calamity [of the evil nations] is near, and future events are rushing at them."[23] When the evildoers will be destroyed, the wonderful promises that Hashem gave Israel will immediately be fulfilled.

This may be likened to a king who was riding on the road with a friend and an enemy. The king became thirsty. The enemy said, "We are far from water," in order to distress him, while the friend said, "Your majesty, ride on, for the water is near us," in order to restore his soul.

Similarly, Bilaam, the foe, said that our salvation is far off. But our friend said, "Keep justice and do charity, for My salvation is soon to come...."[24]

If we overcome Bilaam's accusations, Moshe's prayer for a speedy redemption will be fulfilled.

TENTS OF TORAH AND FRAGRANT SPICES

"*Mah tovu ohalecha Yaakov,* How good are your tents, O Yaakov.... Stretching out like brooks, like gardens by a river, like *ahalim* planted by Hashem...."[25]

When Bilaam tried to curse the Jews, Hashem twisted his tongue so that he blessed them instead, as it is written, "Hashem,

---

23. Devarim 32:35.
24. Yeshayahu 56:1.
25. Bamidbar 24:5–6.

your God, switched the curse to a blessing for you."[26] The Gemara[27] teaches that from what he said, we can deduce what he wanted to say.

The Gemara says,[28] that his blessing, "How good are your tents, O Yaakov," alludes to our shuls and houses of Torah study, as in "Yaakov was a perfect man, abiding in tents."[29]

Blessing lies in our appreciating these "tents," which are so good for us, for only if we appreciate them can we obtain full benefit from them. Failure to appreciate them is a curse.

Bilaam continued to speak of brooks and *ahalim*, which means either "fragrant spices" or "tents."[30] Says the Gemara:[31] Why are tents next to "brooks"? To teach that just as brooks raise a person [who immerses himself in them] from impurity to purity, so do the tents [of Torah study] raise a person from guilt to merit.

What is the connection between "tents" of Torah study and fragrant spices?

Says the Mishnah:[32] "These are the precepts whose fruits a person eats in this world but whose principal remains intact for him in the world to come." The list includes honoring parents, doing acts of kindness, making peace between people, and Torah study which is equivalent to them all.

The Rambam[33] explains that all mitzvot bring reward in the world to come, but mitzvot between man and his fellow also bring one benefit in this world, for people will learn from him to behave

---

26. Devarim 23:6.
27. *Sanhedrin* 105b.
28. *Sanhedrin* 105b.
29. Bereshit 25:27.
30. See Rashi here, and on *Berachot* 16a.
31. *Berachot* 16a.
32. *Pe'ah* 1.
33. Commentary on the Mishnah.

better. And Torah study is equivalent to them all, for it leads to doing mitzvot.

In other words, interpersonal mitzvot are like eating fruit; they're enjoyable in this world. For they win for the one who does them admiration and affection.

As mentioned before, from what Bilaam said, we learn what he wanted to say. From "like gardens by a river," the Gemara learns that he did not want Jews to have olive trees and vineyards.

Evidently Bilaam did not mind if Jews had avocados or mangoes, he only cared if they grew olives and grapes. Why?

Olive oil does not mix with other liquids, always remaining apart and above. Bilaam didn't want the Jews to remain apart like olive oil, he wanted them to mix with the gentiles, assimilate, and disappear. Thus he advised Balak to lead the Jewish men astray with immorality.[34]

The grapevine needs a supportive framework on which to grow. The Jewish family is likened to a grapevine, as in the verse, "Your wife will be like a fruitful grapevine...,"[35] and the Torah is its supportive framework.

The qualities of staying apart from the gentiles and building a Jewish family come from studying Torah, which leads to doing mitzvot. A Jewish man learns in the *bet midrash* until his fragrance spreads for others to enjoy. Thus *ahalim* refers to fragrant spices as well as to tents of Torah.

"Like the fragrance of good oils...."[36] The Gemara says:[37] The Torah scholar resembles a flask filled with spikenard ointment, whose fragrance spreads only if the flask is open — meaning that

---

34. See *Sanhedrin* 106a.
35. Tehilim 128:3.
36. Shir HaShirim 1:3.
37. *Avodah Zarah* 35b.

he teaches Torah to others, as Rashi explains. Bilaam wanted to curse us that scholars would be unwilling to teach others, in which case the Torah would not be transmitted to the next generation.

The Hovot HaLevavot,[38] citing the verse "I will teach sinners Your ways,"[39] adds that a *baal teshuvah*[40] has a special obligation to teach others Hashem's ways in order to rectify his own past. After he has studied the Torah, which refines his personality and gives him a good fragrance, he should spread it to others.

ZIMRI CONFRONTS MOSHE

Moshe said to the judges of Israel, "Let each man kill his men who were attached to Baal Peor."

Behold, a man of the Children of Israel came and brought a Midianite woman near to his brother before the eyes of Moshe and before the eyes of the whole assembly of the Children of Israel; and they were weeping at the entrance of the Tent of Meeting.

Pinehas, the son of Elazar, the son of Aaron HaKohen, saw, and he arose... and took a spear in his hand....[41]

Even after Hashem turned Bilaam's curses into blessings, the forces of impurity did not give up the war against us. Bilaam told Balak, "Come, I will advise you."[42] He said, "The God of Israel detests immorality. I will give you some advice. The Jews like linen garments. Make booths for selling linen. Put an old woman outside the booth and a young one inside...."[43] And Bilaam unfolded

---

38. *Shaar Teshuvah.*
39. Tehilim 51:15.
40. One who repents of his sins.
41. Bamidbar 25:3.
42. Bamidbar 24:14.
43. *Sanhedrin* 106a.

a detailed plan for gradually luring Jewish men from shopping to drinking wine to immorality and idolatry.

Jewish men fell into the trap, and Hashem brought a plague upon Israel.

The plague was for the sin of idolatry, as the Torah states, "Israel became attached to Baal Peor, and Hashem's wrath flared up against Israel."[44] Zimri then sinned with immorality by taking Cozbi, and Pinehas killed him stopping the plague. Since the plague came because of idolatry, why did the plague end when Pinehas killed Zimri and stopped the immorality?

This is all the more puzzling in light of the Gemara,[45] which relates that the Tribe of Shimon went to their leader, Zimri, and said, "They are trying capital cases, and you sit in silence?" Zimri gathered 24,000 of Israel, took Cozbi, and brought her before Moshe. "Son of Amram," he said, "Is this one forbidden or permitted? If you say, 'Forbidden,' who permitted Yitro's daughter to you?"

Accordingly, Zimri staged a big demonstration. What was he trying to accomplish?

The Brisker Rav *zt"l* explains that Zimri was saying: We must be lenient and compromise to prevent something even worse from happening. If our men go to the Midianite camp, they will sin with Midianite women and worship idols. It would be better to bring the Midianite girls into our camp to prevent our men from worshiping idols.

Accordingly, we may explain that when Zimri said, "If you say 'Forbidden,' who permitted Yitro's daughter to you?," he knew very well that Moshe married Yitro's daughter before the Torah was given and converted her. And he knew that taking Yisro's daughter

---

44. Bamidbar 25:5–7.
45. *Sanhedrin* 82a.

was no comparison to sinning with Cozbi. However, Zimri was saying: Your father, Amram, was the distinguished leader of the Jewish people in Egypt. As such, you should have married a wife from a distinguished family, not the daughter of a priest who converted. But since you had no choice, you compromised. Now, we, too, must compromise.

But there is no room for such compromises. The Torah cannot be saved by uprooting part of it.

*   *   *

When Zimri staged his demonstration, Moshe, Aaron, and the judges wept. Why?

I would suggest that Zimri forcefully stopped the judges from sentencing the men of his Tribe to death — and Moshe, Aaron, and the judges wept over the catastrophe they knew would ensue. For our Sages said: When justice is not done on earth, it is done in heaven. The earthly court is extremely restricted; it cannot give the death sentence unless the accused was warned in advance and two eyewitnesses testify against him. The heavenly court is not bound by these restrictions. Indeed, the plague claimed 24,000 lives.

The Gemara continues: Pinehas flung Zimri and Cozbi down before Hashem and said, "Shall 24,000 of Israel die because of these?"

Pinehas was saying: With Zimri out of the way, the earthly courts will be able to execute justice, and once they execute justice the heavenly court will refrain from executing justice and the plague will stop.

Thus by killing Zimri for immorality, the plague which came because of idolatry was stopped.

PARASHAT

Pinehas

PINEHAS IS REWARDED

Pinehas son of Elazar son of Aaron HaKohen turned back My
wrath from the Children of Israel when he was zealous for My
sake... so that I did not annihilate the Children of Israel... Therefore say: Behold, I give him My covenant of peace.

And it shall be for him and his offspring after him a covenant
of eternal priesthood because he was zealous for his God and he
atoned for the Children of Israel.[1]

For boldly slaying Zimri and Cozbi, Pinehas was given two
rewards.

One was "my covenant of peace," which Seforno explains to
mean: Peace from the angel of death. And indeed Pinehas lived an
extremely long time, in fact, he was still alive in the days of Yiftah.
And according to the opinion that Pinehas is Eliyahu HaNavi, he
lives forever.

The other reward was "a covenant of eternal priesthood." Rashi
explains: Although Elazar, Pinehas' father, was a Kohen, since
Pinehas was born before his father was anointed, he did not inherit
the priesthood, and only became a Kohen when he killed Zimri.

---

1. Bamidbar 25:11–13.

The Ohr HaHayyim asks: Why does the Torah state the reason for the rewards twice?

To answer the question, let's examine what took place.

At the end of the previous Parashah, the Torah relates that Jewish men sinned with the daughters of Moav and went astray after their gods. As a result, 24,000 people died in a plague before it was halted when Pinehas speared Zimri and Cozbi.[2]

In Tehilim, we find: "Pinehas rose and *vayefallel*, and the plague was halted."[3] *Vayefallel* can mean, "prayed," "executed judgment," or "argued." Pinehas did all three.

The Gemara[4] says that Pinehas argued with his Creator, flinging Zimri and Cozbi down before Hashem and saying, "Shall 24,000 of Israel die because of these?"

The ministering angels wanted to knock him down, but Hashem said to them, "Let him be. He is a zealot descended from a zealot, an appeaser of Divine wrath descended from an appeaser of Divine wrath."

Rashi explains that he descended from Levi, who was zealous in the incident of Dinah saying, "Shall he treat our sister like a harlot?"[5] And he is descended from Aaron, who halted the plague following Korah's rebellion. Pinhas also did two such things: He was zealous about an act of immorality. And he halted the plague by arguing, "Shall 24,000 of Israel die because of these?"

Halting the plague meant fighting the angel of death and stopping him from doing his job — a dangerous undertaking that required *mesirut nefesh*.[6] In Korah's time, Aaron — Pinehas'

2. Bamidbar 25:9.
3. Tehilim 106:30.
4. *Sanhedrin* 82b.
5. Bereshit 34:31.
6. Self-sacrificing dedication to the point of giving up one's life.

grandfather — had fought the angel of death with *mesirut nefesh*; and the angel refused to stop until Aaron brought him to the Mishkan.[7] Pinehas, too, fought the angel of death with *mesirut nefesh;* and only by a miracle was he saved from the angels who wanted to knock him down.

In addition, Pinehas was zealous about the desecration of Hashem's Name that takes placed when there is immorality, as Pinehas' ancestor Levi said, "Shall he treat our sister like a harlot?" The tribe of Levi's zealotry for the desecration of Hashem's Name at the incident of the golden calf earned the Levites the privilege of serving in the Temple. Similarly, Pinehas earned the privilege of being a Kohen "because he was zealous for his God."

This explains why Pinehas received a twofold reward. For turning back Divine wrath, Pinehas was given peace from the angel of death, and for being zealous regarding immorality, he was granted priesthood.

Pinehas had special qualities and merits which he received from his ancestors, that allowed him to do his great deed and prevented the angels from knocking him down. From here we learn a fundamental principle: When we exert ourselves in a special way to serve Hashem, we plant that quality and its merit into our descendants for their benefit.

TELL EVERYONE

Therefore say: Behold, I give him (Pinehas) My covenant of peace.[8]

Why did Hashem tell Moshe, "Therefore say" — that is, publicize this matter?

---

7. See Bamidbar 17:15; Rashi, Bamidbar 17:13.
8. Bamidbar 25:12.

The Midrash says that after Pinehas slew Zimri the Tribes began to mock him, saying that his mother was a descendent of Yitro, also known as Putiel, as the Torah says, "Elazar son of Aaron took for himself from the daughters of Putiel as a wife."[9] The Tribes said, "Look at this son of Puti. His mother's father fattened calves for idolatry — and he killed the prince of a Tribe in Israel!"

From here it seems that all of the Tribes — even the Tribe of Levi — thought Pinehas was wrong in killing Zimri.

Hashem wanted to declare publicly that Pinehas was right, because the people did not realize what he accomplished on High and that he stopped the angel of death. "Therefore say" — make known that Pinehas turned back My wrath and saved thousands of lives. And for this, "I give him My covenant of peace" — long life.

COUNTING THE PEOPLE

It was after the plague — Hashem spoke to Moshe..., saying: Take a census [literally: lift the head] of the entire congregation of the Children of Israel.[10]

Says Rashi: The matter may be likened to a shepherd whose flock was attacked by wolves. Afterward he counts the sheep to know how many are left.

But what benefit is there in knowing how many sheep are left after the attack by the wolves, or how many Jews were left after the plague? Also, why weren't the Jews counted after the plague in Korah's time?

One more question: Why are Zimri and Cozbi named here and described as prominent people?

---

9. Shemot 6:25.
10. Bamidbar 26:1–2.

I suggest one answer to all these questions.

In Korah's time, the people were stricken because they said to Moshe Rabbenu, "You have killed Hashem's nation,"[11] and the plague was able to set things straight. However, in the incident of Zimri and Cozbi the plague was not sufficient.

Let's examine what happened here.

The Jewish people had always safeguarded their moral purity — even in Egypt, the world center of immorality. Now, suddenly, the fence was breached. Since prominent people were involved, it seemed acceptable. Shame vanished, and the holiness of the Jewish people plummeted. To show the lowliness and ugliness of the deed, Pinehas went around the entire camp of Israel carrying the two aloft on a spear.

Hashem said, "*Si'uh es rosh* — Take a head count — however this can be also be translated as lift the head — of the entire congregation" — count them in order to restore their honor and greatness, and return them to the level of Israel, who are marked by three characteristics: They are compassionate, do acts of kindness, and have a sense of shame.[12]

THE HONEY JAR AND THE SNAKE

Pinehas... turned back My wrath....[13]

The Gemara[14] relates that Rabban Yohanan ben Zakai left besieged Jerusalem to speak to the Roman general Vespasian. When the Sage reached the Roman camp, he said to him, "Peace to you, O king!"

---

11. Bamidbar 17:6.
12. *Yevamot* 79a.
13. Bamidbar 25:13.
14. *Gittin* 56a.

"If I am a king," countered Vespasian, "why didn't you come to me before?"

"The rebellious faction did not let me," said the Sage.

He was referring to the *biryonim,* who had seized control of Jerusalem and insisted on continuing to fight the Romans, disobeying the Sages' ruling that the city should surrender.

Said Vespasian, "If a snake is coiled around a honey jar, does one not break the jar to get rid of the snake?" (Rashi explains: Why didn't you destroy Jerusalem in order to get rid of the rebellious faction?)

Rabban Yohanan ben Zakai was silent.

Rabbi Akiva[15] said: He should have replied, "One takes a pair of tongs, removes the snake and kills it, and leaves the jar intact." (Rashi explains: We were hoping to remove the rebellious faction without destroying Jerusalem.)

Then Vespasian said, "Make a request of me, and I will grant it."

Rabban Yohanan ben Zakai said, "Give me Yavneh and its scholars, the family chain of Rabban Gamaliel, and physicians to heal Rabbi Tzadok."

Rabbi Akiva[16] said: He should have replied, "Let the Jews off this time."

But Rabban Yohanan ben Zakai thought that Vespasian would not grant such a large request, and had he dared ask for it, nothing would have been saved.

This was the dialogue as brought in the Gemara. But there's a big question here — according to the Midrash,[17] Rabban Yohanan ben Zakai did, in fact answer to Vespasian as Rabbi Akiva suggested, but Vespasian refused his request! If so, why does the Gemara say that Rabbi Akiva criticized him?

---

15. According to a different opinion, it was Rabbi Yoseph.
16. According to a different opinion, it was Rabbi Yoseph.
17. Echah Rabbah 1:31.

We may answer that Rabbi Akiva was not criticizing Rabban Yohanan ben Zakai's response to Vespasian but he was criticizing Rabban Yochana's response to Hashem.

Because sometimes Hashem sends a message through a gentile, as in the story of the gentile repairman who asked a Jew, "Have you anything to fix?"

"No," replied the Jew.

"You do have what to fix," said the repairman, "but you don't want to fix it."

The Jew took this as a Divine message that he should mend his ways.

So too, when Vespasian said, "If a snake is coiled around a honey jar, does one not break the jar to get rid of the snake?", Rabban Yohanan ben Zakai heard a Divine message: Hashem planned to destroy Jerusalem and the Temple in order to get rid of the *biryonim* and the Sadducees.

Rabban Yohanan ben Zakai, in view of the wickedness of those factions, accepted Hashem's decree, keeping silent and not arguing with Hashem.

Pinehas, in contrast, refused to accept Hashem's decree. "Pinehas rose and *vayefallel*" — prayed and argued — "and the plague was halted."[18] He flung Zimri and Cozbi down before Hashem and said, "Shall 24,000 of Israel die because of these?"[19]

As the Klausenberger Rebbe *zt"l* said in the name of the Chozeh (Seer) of Lublin: "You shall not do *ken – thus -* to Hashem, your God."[20] But the word *ken* can also be translated as "yes," thus the verse can mean: Don't say, *yes,* to Hashem's decrees! Pray and nullify them, as Moshe Rabbenu did!

---

18. Tehilim 106:30.
19. *Sanhedrin* 82b.
20. Devarim 12:4

Rabbi Akiva maintained that Rabban Yohanan ben Zakai should not have been silent in the face of Hashem's decree. He should have prayed and argued with Hashem, asking Him to wait patiently for the grip of the *biryonim* to weaken, as it surely would, for evil does not last forever.

But since the past cannot be changed, why did Rav Akiva criticize what Rabban Yohanan ben Zakai had already done?

Rabbi Akiva foresaw that in the future, too, an era would come when the Torah Sages no longer rule the people — as is the situation today.

In Jerusalem today, the snake is after the honey — they are fighting the Torah, which is sweeter than honey, and want to take the students of Torah out of the yeshivot.

Since the Halachah is always in accordance with the last-cited opinion in the Gemara, we follow Rabbi Akiva's opinion. We must pray and ask Hashem to wait patiently while we weaken the power of the Other Side by expanding our Torah schools, yeshivot, and kollelim. And it works; we see that many non-observant Jews are returning to the Torah.

We must increase the *kedushah*,[21] and ultimately it will win over the *tumah*.[22] Then the snake's grasp will be removed, and the honey jar will remain intact.

SHEMINI ATZERET

[After the seven days of Sukkot,] On the eight day, you shall have an *atzeret* (gathering; restriction; stopping)....[23]

---

21. Holiness.
22. Impurity.
23. Bamidbar 29:35.

Rashi[24] comments: Tarry with Me a little. This is an expression of affection, as when children are about to take leave of their father and he tells them, "It is difficult for me to part with you. Stay one more day."

Now, how does staying one more day make the parting any easier? Besides, do the Jews part with Hashem when they go home after the festival? After all, the whole earth is filled with His glory!

I would answer as follows. The Jewish people had just spent seven days of Sukkot in Jerusalem, next to the Bet HaMikdash,[25] where they had imbibed a great deal of fear of Heaven and had ascended to a very high spiritual level. Upon returning home, they were liable to descend from this level.

So they remained one more day, spending it together with Hashem for Simhat Torah, because in the Land of Israel, this day is not only Shemini Atzeret but also Simhat Torah. On this day, we celebrate the completion of the weekly Torah readings and begin again from Bereshit, to affirm that we cleave to the Torah and never finish with it. One need only see the men and boys dancing in a yeshiva on Simhat Torah to know how rejoicing over the Torah uplifts us, and provides spiritual fuel to keep us going until the next holiday.

When the day is celebrated in this way, there is no parting with Hashem. In fact, Shemini Atzeret, can be literally translated, "the eighth that stops," for indeed, it stops the parting, and helps us take all the spirituality we acquired over the festival of Sukkot into the new year and into our homes.

---

24. Bamidbar 29:36.
25. Temple.

IF I FORGET THEE, O JERUSALEM

On the Seventeenth of Tamuz, the walls of Jerusalem were breached in the era of the Second Temple. On the Ninth of Av, fire was set to the Temple. We fast on the first date over Jerusalem's destruction and on the second over the Temple's. These are two separate destructions; even if the Temple were standing today in Bnai Brak, we would fast on the Seventeenth of Tamuz over the destruction of Jerusalem.

One of our greatest Sages, who lived through these destructions, was Rabbi Akiva. The Gemara[26] relates that when he married Rahel, they were so poor that they lived in a shed used to store straw. In the morning, Rabbi Akiva would remove the straw from her hair and promise her that when he had money, he would make her a "Jerusalem of gold."

This was a very unusual ornament, as may be deduced from elsewhere in the Gemara.[27] Why did he promise her a Jerusalem of gold, rather than a pearl necklace or diamond ring?

To answer this question, let's study the city's name.

Yerushalayim, as it is called in Hebrew, means "a pair of Yerushalems,"[28] for there is a heavenly Jerusalem and an earthly one. Additionally, the Midrash[29] relates that Hashem combined the names given to it by two *tzaddikim* and called the place Yerushalem.

Shem had called it Shalem, as it is written, "Malki Tzedek [that is, Shem] king of Shalem... a Kohen of God.... blessed [Avraham]...."[30] *Shalem* means "whole" or "perfect." Shem, the son of Noah, had

---

26. *Nedarim* 50a.
27. *Shabbat* 29a.
28. As in *yadayim,* "two hands."
29. *Bereshit Rabbah* 56.
30. Bereshit 14:18–19.

seen mankind wiped out in the Flood for trampling on one another. Perhaps He built the city calling it Shalem hoping that people would respect and appreciate one another and thus there would be *shalem* in the realm of interpersonal relationships.

To this, Avraham Avinu added the name *Yireh* – to see – hoping that the city would epitomize trust in Hashem. On the way to the Akedah,[31] Yitzhak had said, "Here are the fire and the wood, but where is the lamb for the burnt offering?"[32] Avraham replied, "God will see (*yireh*) to the lamb for the burnt offering."[33]

On the Temple Mount, Avraham bound Yitzhak and then released him by Divine command. Then Hashem caused a ram to get caught in the brush so that Avraham could sacrifice it. Avraham named the place Hashem Yireh, "Hashem will see,"[34] both as a description and a prayer. Avraham was describing a place where Hashem sees to everything, even a ram for an offering. He also prayed that whoever trusts in Hashem would see salvation there.

Rabbi Akiva and his wife lived in dire poverty. When he removed the straw from his wife's hair, he told her, "In the end, everything will work out well, and I will make you a Jerusalem of gold as testimony that Hashem sees to everything and brings salvation."

Eventually Rabbi Akiva became very wealthy, as the Gemara continues, and he kept his promise. The *Yerushalmi*[35] relates that the wife of Rabban Gamliel, the Nassi, wanted a Jerusalem of gold, too. Rabban Gamliel said to his wife, "Did you pass all the tests that she did?"

---

31. The Binding of Yitzhak.
32. Bereshit 22:7.
33. Bereshit 22:8.
34. Bereshit 22:14.
35. Daf 34a.

From here we deduce that the Jerusalem of gold was not just an ornament, but a diploma. Rahel had lived in poverty and sent her husband away to learn Torah for twenty-four years; she had successfully withstood difficult trials with supreme *mesirut nefesh*. She was awarded a diploma certifying that she had passed the test of trusting in Hashem.

Trust in Hashem is part of Jerusalem's name and also part of its beauty, as the Gemara[36] says: "Ten measures of beauty came down to the world; Jerusalem took nine of them," and "Whoever did not see Jerusalem in its splendor never saw a beautiful city." Proof comes from the passage:[37] "Great is Hashem and much praised in the city of our God, mount of His Holiness, most beautiful of sites, joy of all the earth..."

Says the Midrash:[38] A booth for accounting was outside of Jerusalem, and whoever wanted to calculate his profits and losses went there. Why was it necessary to go out of Jerusalem to do this? Because if he found that he had lost money, he might become distressed, and one does not get distressed in Jerusalem, for it was the "most beautiful of sites, joy of all the earth."

Joy comes from trusting that Hashem Yireh — Hashem sees to everything.

---

36. *Kiddushin* 49b.
37. *Tehilim* 48:2–3.
38. *Shemot Rabbah, Pikkudei* 52:5.

PARASHAT

Mas'ei

FORTY-TWO JOURNEYS

Moshe wrote their goings out (*motza'eihem*) according to their journeys by the word of Hashem....[1]

Citing Tanhuma, Rashi likens the matter to a king whose son was sick. The king took him to a distant place to heal him. On the way back, his father began to enumerate all their journeys and told him, "Here we slept; here we were cooled; here your head hurt." Similarly, Hashem said to Moshe: Enumerate all the places where they angered me.

Accordingly, we might translate *motza'eihem* as "their happenings."[2]

Taking a closer look at the parable, we see that the Jews coming out of Egypt were like a person with a disease; to rid it of the disease, they were taken on a journey. During their many decades in Egypt, the Jews had absorbed into their souls many "germs". With every journey through the desert, another germ of Egypt was removed.

Accordingly, we might translate *motza'eihem* as "what was removed from them."

---

1. Bamidbar 33:2.
2. Literally, "what found them," as in Devarim 31:17.

The first journey began "on the day after the Pesach offering."[3] The Zohar says that they roasted the Egyptian deity, sending the aroma of barbecued lamb wafting throughout Egypt, and they threw the bones, which they were forbidden to break, intact into the garbage. All this disconnected them from the folly of worshiping the lamb.

Then "the Children of Israel went forth with an upraised hand before the eyes of all Egypt. And the Egypt were burying... every firstborn, and on their god, Hashem had inflicted punishments."[4] Here Hashem removed the Jews' submission to the Egyptians and their admiration of Egypt's idolatry. He gathered them all together in a miraculously short time, as it is written, "I carried you on eagle's wings and brought you to Me."[5] And He implanted in them the joy of "My firstborn son is Israel."[6]

Then "they encamped in Sukkot."[7] Says Targum Yonatan: Here Hashem enveloped them in the seven Clouds of Glory.

In every journey, they learned a new lesson. For instance, "They journeyed from Marah and arrived in Elim; in Elim there were twelve springs of water and seventy date palms."[8] Says Targum Yonatan: The twelve springs corresponded to the Twelve Tribes; and the seventy date palms to the seventy elders of Israel. This taught that from its creation Hashem planned the world for the sake of the Jewish people.

In several places, they angered Hashem, and then repented and became spiritually stronger, in keeping with the verse, "Because I

---

3. Bamidbar 33:3.
4. Bamidbar 33:3–4.
5. Shemot 19:4.
6. Shemot 4:22.
7. Bamidbar 33:5.
8. Bamidbar 33:9.

fell, I rose."[9] Indeed, we often see *baalei teshuvah*[10] who are spiritually stronger than Jews religious from birth.

The Tanhuma continues: Why did the Torah record all of these journeys? Because all these places will ultimately be rewarded by Hashem, as it is written, "The desert... will rejoice...; the dry place will blossom like a lily."[11] If the desert is rewarded for hosting the Jewish people, all the more so one who hosts a Torah scholar in his home!

Moreover, every place has different qualities. On the verse "Israel dwelt in Shitim, and the people began to go astray after the daughters of Moav,"[12] the Tanhuma says: Some fountains grow strong people; others, weak ones. Some grow modest ones; others, immoral ones. The fountain of Shitim was one of immorality.

In other words, Hashem created the world so that every situation and place, even a desert, has a lesson to teach and presents a mission for us to fulfill. In some places and situations, we need to absorb the good. The mission of a Torah scholar's host, for instance, is to cleave to the scholar and learn Torah and good deeds from him. Some places and situations arouse a powerful negative urge, where our mission is to not let ourselves be swept along by it.

Moshe Rabbenu recorded these journeys at the end of the forty years in the desert to teach us that we must review the lessons that we learned in each place, just as one reviews the tractate he has learned after the semester ends. As Moshe said: "You shall remember the whole road on which Hashem, your God, led you these forty years in the desert."[13]

9. Michah 7:8.
10. People who are new to Torah observance.
11. Yeshayahu 35:1.
12. Bamidbar 25:1.
13. Devarim 8:2.

Just as Hashem planned journeys for the Children of Israel in the desert, so does He plan journeys for each of us in this world. Wherever we find ourselves, we have an opportunity to shape our lives for the good. We are able to see Hashem's wonderful *hashgahah*,[14] to learn from our mistakes, and — in the month of Elul — to review the lessons of the past year so that we will not forget them.

This thought enhances the plain meaning of the passage: "Moshe wrote their goings out (*motza'eihem*) according to their journeys." They were like students in school progressing from one grade to the next; after internalizing the lesson of one place, they went on to learn the lesson of the next place.

My life, too, has led me from place to place — from Morocco to London to the Lakewood Yeshiva to Pennsylvania to Saint Louis to Toronto and now to Jerusalem, with many more stops along the way. Looking back, I can say that I received a great deal from each place.

SETTLING THE LAND

You shall possess the Land and you shall settle in it, for to you have I given the Land to possess it.[15]

The Ramban[16] says that we are commanded in many verses to possess the Land and settle in it, and not abandon it to another nation or to desolation. In fact, he counts *yishuv ha'aretz*[17] as one of the 613 mitzvot of the Torah. However, the Rambam seems to disagree for he does not mention this in the *Yad HaHazakah*.

They both agree that it is important not to leave the King's palace desolate, and that even in its desolation, it is holy, so that if

---

14. Providence.
15. Bamidbar 33:53.
16. See Commentary on the Torah and *Sefer HaMitzot*.
17. Settling the Land.

a Jew buys any part of the Land from a gentile, the contract may be written by a gentile on Shabbat. And the Gemara[18] says many wonderful things about the Land, for instance, he who walks four cubits in the Land is assured of the world to come; and whoever is buried in the Land is as if he was buried under the Altar.

However, the Gemara[19] also states that we are bound by oath not to return from the exile. Since Shelomo HaMelech says three times in Shir HaShirim: "I adjure you, O daughters of Jerusalem... not to wake or rouse the love until it pleases,"[20] we learn three oaths. These "oaths" may be understood as strong requests, demands, advice, and guidance. One oath is that the Jewish people not rebel against the nations, rather to accept their authority. The second oath is that they not to go up to the Land "like a wall" — together, by force, fortifying their settlements by building walls around them — unless the nations permit it, as the Maharsha explains. The third is that the nations not subjugate the Jewish people with excessive harshness.

Because of the "oaths," it is impossible to require all Jews to go up to the Land until Mashiah comes. But individuals and groups have done it, such as the disciples of the Vilna Gaon and those of the Baal Shem Tov, as well as many families who went up to make the desolate places bloom and to bring satisfaction to Hashem.

Even if today we do not have a mitzvah to settle the Land, we do have a different mitzvah connected with it. For the Hayyei Adam,[21] citing Sefer Haredim, says: A person should eagerly await the opportunity to fulfill a mitzvah, as it is written, *Ushemartem laasatom,*[22]

---

18. *Ketubot* 111a.
19. *Ketubot* 111a.
20. *Shir HaShirim* 2:7, 3:5; 5:8, 8:4.
21. Part 1 68:15.
22. Devarim 5:1.

"Wait eagerly to do them." Similarly, *shamar* is used to describe Yaakov Avinu's eagerly awaiting the fulfillment of Yosef's dreams.[23]

Accordingly, now we can await the opportunity of fulfilling the mitzvah of settling the Land with the coming of Mashiah, and this awaiting comes to life more if we do it in the Land. Those who live in the Land of Israel today are at least fulfilling the mitzvah of "awaiting."

To speed up the coming of Mashiah, let's study the well-known story of Kamtza and Bar Kamtza.

KAMTZA AND BAR KAMTZA

The Gemara[24] states that Jerusalem was destroyed because of Kamtza and Bar Kamtza. It relates that someone made a feast in his house, to which he invited the Sages of Jerusalem. He sent a messenger to bring his friend Kamtza, but the messenger brought his enemy Bar Kamtza instead.

The host found Bar Kamtza sitting in his house and demanded that he leave. Bar Kamtza pleaded with the host not to shame him, even offering to pay for the whole feast.

But the host refused. He grabbed Bar Kamtza by the hand and showed him the door.

Bar Kamtza then went to the Roman emperor and cunningly convinced him that the Jews had rebelled against him.

The Gemara[25] concludes: "See how great is the power of shame! For Hashem helped Bar Kamtza, and He destroyed His House and burned His Temple."

---

23. Bereshit 37:11.
24. *Gittin* 55b.
25. *Gittin* 57a.

Let's take a fresh look at this episode. Who was Bar Kamtza? And why was the host so insistent that he leave?

Bar Kamtza was far from being a righteous Jew, seen from the fact that he convinced the Roman emperor to come destroy Jerusalem and the Temple, just because he was insulted. I have a feeling that he was a Sadducee, who came to the feast looking for a pretext to make trouble. This is the meaning of the Gemara that says, "Hashem helped Bar Kamtza," for Bar Kamtza was looking for a pretext, and Hashem helped him find one. The destruction had already been decreed, but Hashem brought it about through Bar Kamtza in order to teach us about "the power of shame."

The host had made a feast for the Sages of Jerusalem, who the Gemara[26] calls *neki'ei hadaat,* "clean of mind," because they would only sit at a meal with people they knew because they were careful not to hear *lashon hara,* jesting, off-color jokes, and rubbish that would ruin the purity of their minds.

Evidently these *neki'ei hadaat* did not know Bar Kamtza and had he sat at the feast, they would have had to leave. In other words, by sitting there, Bar Kamtza was ruining the whole feast.

The host thought he was justified in evicting Bar Kamtza, and he could have quoted various sources to prove it. Halachically, a person is permitted to prevent someone from causing him damage or loss.

Accordingly, it would seem that the host was justified in evicting Bar Kamtza to prevent him from ruining his feast.

Except for one thing.

Says the Sefer HaHinuch:[27] Hashem has forbidden to embarrass a Jew, for shame is extremely painful.

---

26. See *Sanhedrin* 23a.
27. Mitzvah 240.

The Gemara[28] states that embarrassing someone publicly is like murdering him. We are required to give up our lives rather than murder someone. But are we required to give up our lives rather than embarrass him? Some Rishonim[29] say yes; others say no.[30] Surely, though, we *are* required to give up everything else rather than embarrass him.

If so, the host was not allowed to save his feast by evicting Bar Kamtza.

Today, too, people often behave like this host. Confident that they are right, perhaps even quoting sources to prove it, they feel justified in attacking other Jews. The Gemara is warning us sternly against such behavior.

"See how great the power of shame is! For Hashem helped Bar Kamtza, and He destroyed His House and burned His Temple."

---

28. *Bava Metzia* 58b.
29. Early Authorities.
30. See Tosaphot 10b; Rabbenu Yonah, Shaarei Teshuvah 3:139; Me'iri.

HUMASH

Devarim

Devarim

FROM FATHERS TO SONS

These are the words [of rebuke] that Moshe spoke....[1]

The Torah commands us "You shall surely rebuke your fellow"[2] so that he will stop sinning. But Moshe Rabbenu's rebuke was not to prevent them from sinning! For he rebuked them about the sins of the Spies and Korah, sins that were over and done with. Besides, he was speaking to a new generation. These sins were committed before his listeners were born, or at most, when they were minors.[3] What was the purpose of this rebuke?

We might answer that Moshe's rebuke was not about sin, but about the root causes of sin. One of these is a lack of strong faith and trust in Hashem, as he said, "You have been rebellious against Hashem."[4] Another is the trait of stubbornness, as he said, "You are a stiff-necked people."[5] Similarly, Yaakov rebuked Reuven for his "water-like impetuosity,"[6] and Shimon and Levi for their anger;[7]

---

1. Devarim 1:1.
2. Vayikra 19:17.
3. Under twenty, the age at which a person becomes liable for Divine punishment.
4. Devarim 9:7.
5. Devarim 9:6.
6. Bereshit 49:4.
7. Bereshit 49:6–7.

they should have calmly considered the consequences instead of acting in haste or out of emotion.

Such rebuke is appropriate to deliver also to the sinners' children, for character traits are both inherited and learned at home.

How important it is for parents to fix their own character traits! For these will be transmitted to their descendants.

REBUKE

These are the words [of rebuke] that Moshe spoke to all Israel....[8]

The Midrash[9] quotes three Sages discussing rebuke in their own generation.

Rabbi Tarfon said: No one in this generation can deliver rebuke.

Rabbi Elazar ben Azaryah said: No one in this generation can accept rebuke.

Rabbi Akiva said: No one in this generation knows how to give rebuke.

Remarkably, Moshe Rabbenu was able to deliver rebuke, and his generation was able to accept it.

Rashi, explains that Moshe spoke "to all of Israel", because had Moshe rebuked only some of them, the others would have said, "You heard the son of Amram and did not answer him back? Had we been there, we would have answered him!"

This is puzzling. How could they have answered? Could they deny the facts?

No, but they could have disagreed with Moshe as to the root causes of the sins. Instead of accepting responsibility for their own

8. Devarim 1:1.
9. *Yalkut Shimoni* 789.

flaws, they might have blamed the hardships of the journey, the food they ate, or even Moshe himself.

People are naturally defensive. They try to justify themselves, saying, "Under those circumstances, there was no alternative"; "I was forced into it"; or "I didn't mean to."

Similarly, Adam blamed his wife, saying, "She gave me of the tree (*etz*), and I ate (*va'ochel*)."[10] What kind of justification is that? Therefore the Baal HaTurim, says that *etz* refers to a "stick," and Adam meant to say: "She beat me with the stick until I ate."

And our Sages interpret what Adam said, *va'ochel, to mean that he said,* "I ate, and I will eat in the future." A person is liable to continue eating forbidden fruit in order to prove that he has done nothing wrong. He convinces himself that it is permitted to transgress Hashem's word if he is forced to do so.

So Moshe rebuked the people to uproot any such thoughts, for self-justification is deserving of judgment in and of itself. As Hashem says, "Behold, I am entering into judgment with you because of your saying, "I have not sinned.""[11]

Today, if rebuke does not help, we must at least protest. Otherwise, it looks as if we agree to sin, and such agreement is a desecration of Hashem's Name.

The Gemara[12] discusses failure to protest in connection with the destruction of the First Temple. The prophet Yehezkel[13] records that Hashem told one angel to set a mark on the foreheads of the righteous, and angels of destruction to strike down everyone who did not have the mark.

Suddenly, in the middle of the verse, a turnabout takes place.

---

10. Bereshit 3:12.
11. Yirmiyahu 2:35.
12. *Shabbat* 55a.
13. See Yehezkel 9:4–6.

Hashem orders the angels of destruction to begin from the righteous.

What happened?

The Gemara explains that the attribute of strict justice objected, for the righteous had not protested.

"It is clear to Me," Hashem replied, "that their protests would have been ignored."

"It was clear to You," said the attribute of strict justice, "but it was not clear to them!"

Hashem accepted the argument and instructed the destroyers to strike down both the righteous and the wicked — and to strike the righteous first.

Perhaps Rav Baruch Ber Lebowitz *zt"l* had this in mind when he gathered the students of his yeshiva and said, "I hereby protest the desecration of Shabbat by some Jews in our town."

ON CAMERA

....on the other side of the Jordan, in the desert, in the Aravah, opposite the Reed, between Paran and Tophel and Lavan, and Hatzerot, and Di-zahav.[14]

Rashi explains: Since these are words of rebuke, in which Moshe enumerated all the places where they had angered Hashem, he spoke in hints out of concern for Israel's honor.

How did Moshe expect a riddle to awaken the Jews to repent? Besides, later he delivered all the rebukes in detail, harshly, without concern for their honor!

We might answer that Moshe began by teaching them a concept that was a gentle rebuke.

---

14. Devarim 1:1.

The Gemara[15] states that the stones and beams of a person's house testify to his sin, as it is written, "For a stone will cry out from the wall, and a sliver will answer it from the beams."[16]

That is, any mitzvah or sin that a person does in any place becomes a permanent reality in that place. He is photographed against the scenery as it were, and in the World of Truth, he will see himself within this reality that will testify about him.

Moshe explained that if a person sinned in the Paran Desert, or if Di-zahav (literally: abundant gold) caused him to sin, the sin became a permanent reality that will ultimately testify against him.

Knowing the effect of sin is a rebuke that penetrates deep into a person's consciousness. Still, it is a relatively gentle rebuke couched in hints and a suitable place to begin.

LIKE THE STARS OF HEAVEN

Hashem, your God, has multiplied you and you are today like the stars of heaven in abundance. May Hashem, the God of your forefathers, add to you a thousand times yourselves, and bless you as He has spoken concerning you.[17]

Rashi discusses these two verses. He asks, : Were they "today like the stars of heaven"? They were only 600,000! He answers: They were likened to the day because they will exist forever, like the sun, moon, and stars [which determine the twenty-four-hour cycle of a day[18]].

He asks: Why, after saying, "May Hashem... add to you a thousand

---

15. *Hagigah* 16a.
16. Havakkuk 2:11.
17. Devarim 1:10–11.
18. Siftei Hachamim.

times yourselves," did Moshe add, "and bless you as He has spoken concerning you"?

He answers: Because when he said Hashem will increase you a thousand-fold the Jews objected, saying, "Moshe, are you putting a limit on our blessing? Hashem already promised Avraham, 'If a man can count the dust of the earth, then your offspring, too, will be counted'!"[19] Moshe replied, "This thousand-fold blessing is from me. But Hashem will bless you as He has spoken concerning you."

How did Moshe answer their question? If Hashem blessed them without limit, why would they need Moshe's limited blessing?

We might explain that the entire blessing mentioned here refers not to the quantity of the Jewish people rather to their quality. Moshe said: Having received the Torah and seen so many of Hashem's miracles, you became great like the stars; and your greatness will pass on to your children and your disciples, and to their children and disciples — forever, as Rashi says.

Moshe then continued: Your greatness will increase a thousand times more through fear of heaven and good conduct.

Fear of heaven came to them through Moshe, who instilled in them the understanding that it is oxygen to the soul. Thus he later said "What does Hashem, your God, ask of you, but only to fear Hashem...."[20]

Moshe concluded: What you learned from me has a limit. But what you learn from Hashem does not. Study His ways, for "How great are Your deeds, Hashem; Your thoughts are exceedingly deep."[21] And study His Torah — the revealed part and the Kabbalistic secrets — for Torah is unlimited, and it is the greatest blessing of all.

---

19. Bereshit 13:16.
20. Devarim 10:12.
21. Tehilim 92:6.

PARASHAT

Va'et'hanan

"I'M A HEBREW"

[Hashem had decreed that Moshe could not enter the Land of Israel. Moshe said:] I entreated Hashem at that time, saying, "Let me now cross and see the good Land that is across the Jordan...."[1]

The Midrash[2] says: Moshe offered 515 different prayers, the numerical value of the word, ואתחנן — "I entreated," asking Hashem to rescind the decree and let him enter the Land. Why didn't Moshe also pray for Aaron, who was subject to the same decree? Because he knew that Hashem would not relent, having so decreed with an oath.

If so, why did Moshe pray for himself?

We may answer in light of the following exchange between Moshe and Hashem recorded in the Midrash.

"Master of the world," said Moshe, "Yosef's bones will enter the Land — and I will be unable to do so?!"

Hashem answered, "He who acknowledged his Land will be buried in it; and he who did not, will not. Potiphar's wife called

---

1. Devarim 3:23–25.
2. *Devarim Rabbah* 2 and 11.

Yosef a 'Hebrew man';[3] and he himself said, 'I was kidnapped from the Land of the Hebrews.'[4] But Yitro's daughters referred to you as an Egyptian saying, 'An Egyptian man saved us...'[5]; you heard and were silent, therefore you will not be buried in the Land."

Yosef lived in the Land for only a few years, and Moshe did not live there at all, yet both were expected to have a connection to it, as is every Jew, wherever he lives.

Perhaps since Moshe grew up in Pharaoh's palace and learned the protocol of Egyptian royalty, he had some attachment to Egypt, and therefore there was a Divine criticism of Moshe in this matter.

Moshe offered 515 prayers corresponding to the word "I entreated" in order to express a strong longing for the Land, which Hashem designated for the Jewish people. Moshe asked to enter even as a bird or beast, as if to say: Even that is more of an honor than being a prince in Pharaoh's palace.

Mesilat Yesharim[6] says that we should always long for Jerusalem, feel distress over its disgrace, and pray for the redemption of our people. From the verse "She is Tzion — no one seeks her,"[7] our Sages learn that seeking is required. Let no one think, "Who am I to pray for Jerusalem? Will the redemption sprout because of *my* prayer?" For man was created alone so that each of us would say, "The world was created for me." And it pleases Hashem when His children plead and pray for these things. Even if their request is not granted because the time is not yet ripe or for any other reason, we have done our part and Hashem is happy with this.

Our Sages put several blessings about the redemption into the

---

3. Bereshit 39:13.
4. Bereshit 40:15.
5. Shemot 2:19.
6. Chapter 19, citing *Tanna d'Vei Eliyahu*.
7. Yirmiyahu 30:17.

Amidah because we are obligated to pray for the final redemption and to connect to the Land of Israel. And when we do so, Hashem is happy.

YEARNING

I entreated Hashem at that time, saying, "...Let me now cross and see the good Land that is across the Jordan...."[8]

Asks the Gemara:[9] Why did Moshe yearn to enter the Holy Land? Did he need to eat its fruits? Rather, he said, "There are many mitzvot that can only be fulfilled in the Land of Israel. Let me enter the Land so that I can fulfill them." Hashem said to him, "You only want to enter to receive the reward for fulfilling the mitzvoth, I will consider it as if you have fulfilled them."

The Maharsha asks: How can the Gemara say that Moshe would seek reward, after all the Mishnah[10] says: Be not like servants who serve the master for the sake of receiving a reward?!

We may answer in light of the *Mesilat Yesharim*, which begins: The foundation of piety is that it should be clear to a person what his duty in this world is, and to what he should set his sights and goals all the days of his life. Our Sages taught us that man was created only to delight in Hashem, which is the ultimate enjoyment, and the place for this is in the world to come.

From this we understand that the world to come is not an extraneous reward like a master gives his servant for his work. Rather, the purpose of serving Hashem is to draw one's soul close to Him; as David HaMelech said, "God's closeness is my good."[11] For the

---

8. Devarim 3:23–25.
9. *Sotah* 14a.
10. *Avot* 1:3.
11. Tehilim 73:28.

greatest enjoyment of the soul, which comes from a very high place, is to return to its source. And the world to come is where one is close to Him.

Each mitzvah draws a person closer to Hashem, and Moshe yearned for the closeness that would come from the mitzvot of the Land. Hashem said to him, "Do you want to receive reward — meaning the closeness that comes from these mitzvot?" "I consider it as if you have fulfilled them — meaning your yearning to fulfill these mitzvot itself will draw you close. For, as our Sages teach: If a person planned to fulfill a mitzvah but was prevented from doing so, it is considered as if he fulfilled it.

Desire is an important part of serving Hashem.

THE PRAYER OF MANY

"Yehoshua... shall cause this people to inherit the Land that you will see."

We remained in the valley, opposite Bet Pe'or. And now, Israel, obey the statutes....

Your eyes have seen what Hashem did with Baal Pe'or, that every man who followed Baal Pe'or, Hashem... destroyed him....[12]

Rashi explains that the beginning of the verse, *We remained in the valley, opposite Bet Pe'or,* refers to the idol worship the Bnei Yisrael did in Baal Pe'or. Moshe was saying: You became attached to idolatry, yet Hashem forgave you, as evident by what He said, "And now, Israel, obey the statutes," meaning that all is forgiven. Although you merited forgiveness for your sin, I did not merit forgiveness for my sin and was not permitted to enter the Land.

---

12. Devarim 3:28–4:3.

Did Hashem forgive them for worshiping Baal Pe'or? On the contrary, He destroyed whoever did so!

Besides, Moshe was delivering a rebuke. Where is the rebuke in these words?

Both questions have one answer.

Moshe is speaking not of those who worshipped idols, for they were indeed punished. He was speaking to those who saw them serving idols, for even one who only observes one serving idols is tainted by the sin. As Moshe said later, "We passed through the midst of the nations.... and you saw their detestable idols,"[13] for even seeing idols is very detrimental, as the Torah commands, "You shall not explore after your heart and after your eyes."[14]

Moshe was telling them that Hashem forgave them for looking at the idols. Since there is no forgiveness without repentance and prayer, they surely must have repented and prayed.

Moshe was telling them: Your prayer was accepted, for Hashem does not despise the prayer of the many, however, my prayer, since it was the prayer of an individual, was rejected.

Herein lay an implied rebuke: Why didn't you as a congregation pray for me?

Indeed, the Midrash[15] relates: When Moshe was about to die, since they had not prayed that he enter the Land, he assembled them and began to rebuke them. He said to them, "One redeemed 600,000 — and 600,000 could not redeem one?!"

The prayer of the many has tremendous power.

---

13. Devarim 29:15–16.
14. Bamidbar 15:39.
15. *Devarim Rabbah,* end of Parashat Ki Tavo.

TO LOVE HASHEM

You shall love Hashem, your God, with all your heart, with all your soul, and with all your resources.

And these things that I command you today shall be upon your heart. You shall teach them thoroughly to your children, and you shall speak of them, while you sit in your home, while your walk on the road....[16]

What love are we commanded to have for Hashem?

Rashi, citing the Sifri, says that love of Hashem will come about through keeping, "these things that I command you today... to teach [Torah] to your children, and speak words of Torah," for through this, you will recognize Hashem and cleave to His ways.

But the Rambam, in Hilchot Teshuvah,[17] says: One should love Hashem with an extremely great, strong love, until his soul is attached to love of Hashem, and he is immersed in it always, when he sits down, when he gets up, when he eats.... Thus Shelomo said metaphorically, "I am lovesick,"[18] and all of Shir HaShirim is a metaphor for this matter.

In short, there are two views how love of Hashem is expressed. The Sifri says by studying Torah; the Rambam says by thinking about Him.

The Zohar[19] says that every word of Torah is Hashem's Name; and a person who learns Torah is cleaving to Hashem, for He and the Torah are one. As such, when one learns Torah, he is thinking about Hashem.

Accordingly, there is no contradiction between the Sifri and the

---

16. Devarim 6:5–6.
17. 10:3.
18. Shir HaShirim 2:5.
19. Parashat Emor.

Rambam. When a person studies Torah, he connects to Hashem. He also learns Hashem's ways and cleaves to Him, fulfilling what the Rambam said in Hilchot Yesodei HaTorah:[20]

> This glorious, awesome God — it is a mitzvah to love Him... as it is written, "You shall love Hashem, your God." And what is the way to love of Him? When a person looks into His great, wonderful deeds and creations....

By learning Torah, one sees Hashem's ways and comes to love Him until he reaches the level of "I am lovesick."

Shir HaShirim[21] speaks of *me'ulefet sapirim,* "fainting sapphires." This refers to Torah scholars who are strong like sapphire stones but become faint from long hours of intensive Torah study. The Midrash[22] cites Rabbi Elazar the son of Rabbi Shimon bar Yohai as an example.

Merchants came to buy wheat and lodged in Rabbi Shimon's home leaving their donkeys outside. They saw young Elazar sitting near the oven while his mother baked bread. As she took the loaves out of the oven, he immediately ate them, finishing one tray after another. The merchants said to one another, "He's liable to bring a famine to the world!'

Elazar overheard and was insulted. He took their donkeys, lifted them one at a time, and put them on the roof. When the merchants found out, they complained to Rabbi Shimon. "Did you perhaps offend my son?" he asked.

They told him what happened. "Was he eating your food?" said Rabbi Shimon. "He Who created him also sustains him! Nevertheless, ask him in my name to bring your donkeys down.'"

---

20. Chapter 2:1–2.
21. 5:14.
22. *Shir HaShirim Rabbah* 5:3.

They did as instructed, and Elazar brought down the donkeys — two at a time!

The Midrash continues: But when he studied Torah, he could not bear the weight of his tallit!

To put that much energy in Torah study is possible only if one is lovesick over Hashem and His Torah.

Before we can love Hashem, however, we must love our fellow Jew.

The Gemara[23] relates that a convert came to Hillel asking to learn the Torah on one foot. Hillel taught him the verse "You shall love your friend as yourself."[24]

What a strange request! And what did Hillel mean by his answer?

Evidently the convert was no scoffer, for if he were, there would be no point in Hillel answering him. Rather, the convert was asking for one mitzvah to start with, from which he would get to the whole Torah.

Rashi comments that the mitzvah "You shall love your friend as yourself" applies also to loving Hashem, of Whom it is written, "Forsake not your Friend and your father's Friend."[25]

Accordingly, we might explain that Hillel told the convert: Develop a relationship with a friend, helping him and doing favors for him. He will reciprocate, and you will appreciate what he does for you. This will bring you to come to appreciate all the good that Hashem bestows on you, and you will come to love Hashem. And, as the Rambam says in Hilchot Teshuvah:[26] When a person loves Hashem properly, he will immediately fulfill all the mitzvot out of love.

23. *Shabbat* 31a.
24. Vayikra 19:18.
25. Mishlei 27: 10.
26. Chapter 10:2.

TEFILLIN

Bind them as a sign on your arm and let them be ornaments between your eyes.[27]

When a boy turns thirteen, he becomes obligated in all the mitzvot — yet special emphasis is placed on the mitzvah of *tefillin*. This shows that the mitzvah of *tefillin* contains guidance how one should lead his life.

When the Jewish people accepted Torah and mitzvot, they said, *Naaseh venishma,*[28] "We will do and we will understand." They preceded *Naaseh to venishma* saying that first we will do, and then we will understand.

The two Tefillin, says the Zohar,[29] parallel *naaseh venishma*. The hands do the mitzvoth, while the head understands their inner meaning. Therefore the hand-*tefillin,* which represent *naaseh,* are put on before the head-*tefillin,* which represent *nishma*.

It is told that a professor came to Rabbi Yehezkel Abramsky *zt"l* and said to him, "I would like to start putting on *tefillin*. But please explain their importance."

Rabbi Yehezkel Abramsky said, "First put them on for a month, then come back and I'll tell you."

A month later, the professor came back and said, "You don't need to explain. I've become attached to the *tefillin* and I understand their importance."

How did this happen?

Doing a mitzvah with the right intent has the power to sanctify a person's body, as we say in the blessing over a mitzvah, "Who as sanctified us with His mitzvot and has commanded us...". We

---

27. Devarim 6:8.
28. Shemot 24:7.
29. Parashat Behar.

become so attached to the mitzvah that we feel it's impossible *not* to do it.

Thus the mitzvah of *tefillin* is the foundation of all the mitzvot because it is an echo of *Naaseh venishma*. First we will do [the mitzvah], and then we will understand [its importance].

This has many ramifications.

First we will do the mitzvah, even if we do not yet know the deep intentions behind it. We can make do with saying, "Let this mitzvah be worthy before You as if I fulfilled it with all the intentions." Eventually we will be able to have all these intentions ourselves.

In the blessing of the new month, we ask for "life in which there is fear of heaven," and then we ask for "life in which fear of heaven will be in us." The first is *naaseh* — a person should put himself in an environment — a yeshiva, a religious neighborhood — where there is fear of heaven. The second is *nishma* — we pray that fear of heaven enter us.

First the bar mitzvah boy might study a tractate of Gemara with the straightforward meaning. Then, when he matures, he will study it in depth.

Thus the mitzvah of *tefillin* provides him with guidance for life: *Naaseh venishma!*

SHABBAT NAHAMU

"Comfort, comfort My people," says your God. "Speak to Jerusalem's heart and proclaim to her that her sentence has been completed, that her iniquity has been forgiven; for she has received from Hashem's hand double for all her sins."[30]

---

30. Yeshayahu 40:1–2.

Says the Midrash:[31] She sinned doubly, as it is written, *Het hatah Yerushalim,* literally: "Jerusalem has sinned a sin."[32] She is smitten doubly, as it is written, "She has received from Hashem's hand double for all her sins." And she is comforted doubly, as it is written, "Comfort, comfort My people."

"She sinned doubly" surely refers to quality rather than quantity. Doing a sin with joy and enthusiasm makes it twice as bad.

Thus on Mount Sinai, Hashem told Moshe that some people had made a golden calf. But not until he came down and saw them dancing around it did he break the Tablets.

Similarly, Parashat Ki Tavo warns of terrible curses that come on the Jewish people "because you did not serve Hashem, your God, with joy....."[33] This may be read: "Your failure to serve Hashem was done with joy!

Shelomo HaMelech said, "Don't do a lot of wickedness."[34] The Gemara[35] asks: Is a little okay?!

The Gemara proceeds to explain the warning by comparing sin to eating garlic, which causes an unpleasant odor.

Suppose someone likes garlic, and he has eaten some. He might think, "I already reek of garlic; I might as well eat more."

Shelomo HaMelech says: "Don't do a lot of wickedness" — Use the brakes! Continuing, will make the stench of sin worse and last longer. Stop!

Smoking one cigarette less on Shabbat is a great thing for a non-observant Jew. Stopping in the middle of a quarrel with a spouse has saved marriages.

---

31. *Echah Rabbati,* end of ch. 1.
32. Echah 1:8.
33. Devarim 28:47.
34. Kohelet 7:17.
35. *Shabbat* 31b.

If a person isn't ready to stop sinning, at least he should feel bad that he's doing something wrong. This, too, reduces the wickedness.

Unfortunately, there are some sins we don't feel bad about. Our Sages call them "sins that a person tramples with his heels." Why does he take them lightly? Because any sin committed more than once, begins to feel permitted, making it very hard to repent. Even if one planned to commit a sin but didn't manage to carry out his plan, once he feels the sin is permitted, he is held accountable.

Says Shaarei Teshuvah:[36] We should at least feel distress over sins that we take lightly. Common ones include swearing or mentioning Hashem's Name in vain, cursing, *lashon hara*, groundless hatred, haughtiness, looking at forbidden sights, and wasting time when Torah could have been studied. Anyone who wishes to repent should write a list of his shortcomings in the positive and negative mitzvot, and read it daily.

On Tishah B'Av we promised Hashem, "We will search and examine our ways and return to Hashem."[37] After searching to find our sins, we need to examine whether we did them hesitantly and sadly, or as if they were permitted.

Are we keeping our promise?

It is helpful to read *Pele Yo'etz* (available also in English), which provides wonderful advice about how to serve Hashem.

If we return to Him, our iniquity will be forgiven, and we will be comforted doubly with the rebuilding of Jerusalem speedily in our days.

---

36. 1:5,8.
37. Echah 3:40.

PARASHAT

Ekev

REWARD FOR MITZVOT

Vehayah ekev, This shall be the reward when you obey these laws (*mishpatim*), and you observe them and perform them. Hashem, your God, will keep for you the covenant and the kindness that He swore to your Forefathers. He will love you, bless you, and multiply you....[1]

Ekev, means, "the end result" or, "reward."[2] Literally it also means, "heel" and thus Rashi comments: If you obey the light mitzvot that a person tramples with his heels, Hashem will keep His promise for you.

This refers to the promise to the Forefathers to give us the Land of Israel.

But how can the Torah promise us earthly reward? The Gemara[3] states: There is no reward for mitzvot in this world! Besides, the Mishnah[4] says: Be not like servants who serve the master for the sake of receiving a reward.

We might explain by noting that our verse speaks of obeying

---

1. Devarim 7:12–13.
2. As in Tehilim 19:12; see Baal HaTurim, Ibn Ezra, Ramban.
3. *Kiddushin* 39b.
4. *Avot* 1:3.

mishpatim, which refers specifically to monetary laws, and other laws between man and his fellow, as the Ramban notes. These are often taken lightly, as *Mesilat Yesharim*[5] says: Although most people are not outright thieves, and do not put their hands into other people's pockets, most of them do taste thievery in their business dealings. They permit themselves to delay paying wages, encroach on another's domain, or deal dishonestly.

Mesilat Yesharim[6] continues: Employees who take time from their work for other things are also stealing. Our Sages exempted laborers from blessings and even from Shema; Abba Hilkiyah did not return the Sages' greeting in order not to take time from his employer; and Yaakov Avinu said, "By day I was consumed by the heat and by the frost at night; my sleep fled from my eyes."[7]

Causing any damage is forbidden; even damages for which the earthly court does not punish, the heavenly court does. Littering is one example out of many.

All monetary laws — prohibitions as well as positive commands — benefit society. Parashat Derachim,[8] citing Maharit, says that a person may do mitzvot that benefit others for the sake of reward in this world. Thus the Gemara[9] states that a person who gives charity "so that my son will live" is perfectly righteous. A person who does a mitzvah that benefits others in this world can intend to benefit himself in this world, measure for measure. Doing someone a favor and asking for a reward is acceptable, however, requesting a reward for serving Hashem, Who gives us everything we have, is a chutzpa.

---

5. Chapter 11: *Nekiyut,* "Cleanliness."
6. Chapter 11: *Nekiyut,* "Cleanliness."
7. Bereshit 31:40.
8. *Derech HaAtarim, Derush* 3.
9. *Pesahim* 8a.

It remains to explain how this can be reconciled with the Gemara that says that there is no reward for mitzvot in this world.

The Mishnah[10] says: These are the mitzvot whose fruits a person eats in this world, while the principal remains intact for him in the world to come: honoring father and mother, *gemilut hasadim* (doing acts of kindness), and bringing peace between a man and his fellow. And studying Torah is equivalent to them all.

Tosfot Yom Tov, citing the Rambam, says that the Mishnah is speaking of mitzvot between man and his fellow. When he performs these mitzvot, in addition to the reward in the world to come, he benefits in this world from treating people well. A nice person lives a good life; people like and admire him. As for Torah study, it enables him to know what to do.

The monetary laws are certainly included in *gemilut hasadim*, for by not causing people damage or harm, one is certainly treating them kindly. For this, a person can eat the fruits in this world, but the reward for the mitzvah remains intact for the world to come; it is never given in this world.

The Midrash[11] quotes a conversation between Hashem and the Jewish people concerning reward in this world and the next.

Hashem said, "I have given you Shabbat only for your benefit. You sanctify Shabbat with food, drink, and clean clothes, and enjoy yourself, and I will pay your reward [in the world to come.]"

Thus it is written, "You shall call Shabbat a delight."[12] That is, Hashem gave us the mitzvah of Shabbat so we should have pleasure in this world. And afterward it is written, "Then you will delight in Hashem."[13]

---

10. Pe'ah 1:1.
11. *Devarim Rabbah,* Ekev 1.
12. Yeshayahu 58:13.
13. Yeshayahu 58:14.

The Jewish people asked Him, "And when will You give us the reward for the mitzvot that we fulfill?"

Hashem replied, "You will eat of their fruits now, but the reward I will give you in the end." Thus it is written, *Vehayah ekev,* "It will be at the end...."

WITH JOY

Vehayah ekev tishme'un, It shall be as a reward for obeying these laws....[14]

The Ohr HaHayyim notes that elsewhere the Torah promises reward for mitzvot in a more straightforward way: Parashat Behukotai begins *Im behukotai telechu,* "If you follow my decrees... followed by, "and I will give rain in the proper time"[15] Our Parashah should begin *Im tishme'un,* "If you obey, you shall be rewarded"? Why does it start, "It shall be as a reward"?

Also, Rashi interprets *ekev* as "heel" and explains: If you obey the light mitzvot that a person tramples with his heels, Hashem will keep His promise for you.

Accordingly, the verse could have begun "As reward for the light mitzvot that a person tramples with his heels." Why do we need to begin with the word *vehayah,* "It shall be"?

Our Sages teach that *vehayah* is used in Tanach[16] to denote joy. Accordingly, our verse can be interpreted to mean that mitzvot must be kept with joy.

Unfortunately, many people think that merely performing the mitzvah is enough. They take the joy of a mitzvah as a light matter, and trample it with their heels.

---

14. Devarim 7:12–13.
15. Vayikra 26:3.
16. Scripture.

In truth, joy is a very important part of the mitzvah, as the Rambam[17] states:

> We are commanded about joy, for there is service of the Creator in it, as it is written, "Because you did not serve Hashem, your God, with joy and goodness of heart when everything was abundant."[18] From here you learn that the [correct] service [of Hashem] is with joy.

Rav Baruch Toledano *zt"l* brought this teaching to life. Before eating an apple, he would lift it up in his two hands and say the blessing aloud and joyfully.

GRATITUDE

You shall eat and be satisfied and you shall bless Hashem....[19]

A top American surgeon was flown into Israel to operate on Rav Elyashiv *zt"l*. Since they did not have a common language, any communication between the two went through an interpreter. After the operation, Rav Elyashiv asked to be taught how to say *Todah*[20] in English so that he could thank the surgeon directly.

Why? He cited the Avudraham's comment that in the repetition of the Amidah, the *hazan* says the blessings and we say Amen — until it comes to *Modim,* the expression of gratitude. Here Amen is not enough; we must say *Modim D'Rabbanan* ourselves.

Another proof comes from our verse. The Halachah allows one person to exempt another with the blessings over the mitzvot, but

---

17. *Hilchot Yom Tov* 6:20.
18. Devarim 28:47.
19. Devarim 8:10.
20. Thank you.

not with *Birkat HaMazon*. Our Sages learn from "You shall eat... and you shall bless Hashem" that the one who ate is the one who must thank Hashem.

Why?

Our Sages[21] said that a guest owes his life to the host. That is, a person who receives a benefit from another must feel indebted and show submissiveness to his benefactor. This is possible only if he thanks him face to face.

If we accustom ourselves to thank other people this way, we will do the same for Hashem, to whom we are infinitely indebted. We will say *Birkat HaMazon* with the feeling of "Were our mouth full of song like the sea, and our tongue of joyous song like its multitude of waves, and our lips of praise like the expanse of the heavens... we still could not sufficiently thank You... for even one of the billions of favors that You have done for our ancestors and for us!"[22]

A HUNDRED BLESSINGS A DAY

> Now, O Israel, what (*mah*) does Hashem, your God ask of you? Only to fear Hashem....[23]

There are two types of *yirah* — fear. The lower type, which each of us is obligated in, is fear of sin; we must regard sinning the same way we regard jumping into a fire. The higher level, is awe of Hashem's great glory.

The Gemara[24] asks: The verse says that all Hashem asks from us is to fear Him. Is fear of Hashem really a small thing? The Gemara

---

21. *Shemot Rabbah* 18.
22. The *Nishmat* prayer.
23. Devarim 10:12.
24. *Megillah* 22a.

answers that yes, for Moshe Rabbenu it was indeed a simple thing.

This is puzzling because Moshe was not talking to himself rather to the entire Jewish people, and for them fear of Hashem was not a small thing at all!

We may explain that Moshe was giving the people advice how to acquire fear easily.

Rabbi Meir[25] said: A person is required to recite a hundred blessings each day, as it is written, "What (*mah*) does Hashem, your God ask of you?" Do not interpret *mah, as,* "what," but *me'ah,* "a hundred."[26] Meaning that one should recite one hundred blessings each day.

Everyone followed Moshe's advice and recited a hundred blessings daily to acquire *yirah.* Later, David HaMelech made the practice obligatory in order to stop the hundred untimely deaths that were occurring daily.

Today we all recite a hundred blessings daily — in the prayers, before and after eating or drinking, etc. If so, why isn't *yirah* easy for us?

The question is how we recite the blessings.

A Hassid visited a saintly Rebbe and saw him take an apple, recite a blessing, and eat it. The Hassid was surprised. How was the Rebbe any different from himself?

The Rebbe read his thoughts and said, "I'll tell you the difference between you and me. I want to thank and praise Hashem for His wonderful creation by reciting a blessing, so I eat an apple. But you want to eat an apple, so you recite a blessing."

Evidently the Rebbe recited the blessings as Moshe did, for there is a spark of Moshe in the *tzaddikim* of every generation. If

---

25. *Menahot* 43b.
26. Rashi.

we recite a hundred blessings as Moshe and the Rebbe did, we will acquire fear of heaven.

*　　　*　　　*

Alternatively, Moshe was saying that the effort of acquiring *yirah* is a small thing compared to the result. Moshe was like the man who climbed up a tall mountain, and found a chest filled with gold and diamonds at the peak. He called out exuberantly to the people below, "The effort of climbing the mountain is a small thing compared to the treasure that is up here. Start climbing!"

Indeed, the Gemara[27] compares *yirah* to a treasure, and says: Everything is in the hands of heaven except fear of heaven, as it is written, "Now, O Israel, what (*mah*) does Hashem, your God ask of you? Only to fear Hashem." (Rashi explains: A person's entire situation is dictated by Hashem, except for his fear of heaven. That alone is left to his free choice.) Hashem has nothing in His treasury except the treasure of fear of heaven, as it is written, "Fear of Hashem — that is one's treasure."[28]

BETROTHAL AND MARRIAGE

[The Land of Israel is] a land that Hashem, your God, seeks out....[29]

On our verse, the Sifri says: Hashem seeks out and prospers building and planting, as well as betrothal and marriage, in the Land of Israel.

Why does the Sifri say that betrothal only will prosper in the Land of Israel?"

---

27. *Berachot* 33b.
28. Yeshayahu 33:6.
29. Devarim 11:12.

Does Hashem seek and prosper these things only in the Land of Israel? He prospers them in the whole world!

Our Sages teach that Hashem seeks out the Land of Israel, and other lands only incidentally. Similarly, we might answer that He prospers these things in the Land of Israel, and in other lands only incidentally.

We may ask, why is betrothal mentioned at all? Construction, planting, and marriage are separate and necessary. But betrothal, is merely a temporary state in preparation for marriage!

Surprisingly, the Sifri is teaching us that betrothal is also permanent. Indeed, Hashem promises, "I will betroth you to Me forever."[30]

What permanence is there in betrothal?

Marriage is like building and planting. The new couple will build a home — as we bless them, "May you merit building a faithful home in Israel." They will also plant a vineyard that will yield beautiful fruit. Construction and planting require planning, and the betrothal period is the time for planning the framework in which the couple will live their entire lives.

The Gemara[31] states: "A man who lives without a wife lives without Torah." Although Torah is also studied before marriage, living with Torah — living in accordance with what we have learned — comes after marriage. Then we are constantly challenged to behave with good *midot,* refrain from hurtful words, shower our spouse with *hesed,* and see only the good in him or her.

The engagement period is a time when the couple see only the good in one another. We pray that this situation will endure forever, as in "I will betroth you to Me forever."

---

30. Hoshea 2:21.
31. *Yevamot* 62b.

PARASHAT

Re'eh

IN YOUR HANDS

Re'eh anochi, See, I place before you today blessing and curse.[1]

Why does the Torah tell us to see rather than to listen? Also, usually the Torah uses the word *ani* to say, "I", why does the Torah here use the word, *anochi* ?

We may answer in light of the Midrash Rabbah that says:[2] Starting from the time Hashem said at Sinai, ["I place before you today blessing and curse",] "evil and good do not emanate from the mouth of the Most High."[3] Rather, evil comes automatically to evildoers, and good to doers of good.

Rav Eliyahu Lopian *zt"l* [4] explains that Moshe is telling the Jewish people: Until the Torah was given, Hashem would decree good or evil to the world as He saw fit. After the Torah was given, Hashem placed the management of the world in your hands. If you do evil, you will bring evil upon the world, and if you do good, you will bring good upon the world.

---

1. Devarim 11:26.
2. *Devarim Rabbah* 3.
3. Eichah 3:38.
4. In his *Lev Eliyahu.*

Accordingly, "see" means contemplate the matter. And *Anochi* alludes to *Anochi Hashem Elokecha,* "I am Hashem, your God" — the first of the Ten Commandments, uttered by Hashem when He gave us the Torah. Thus the verse is telling us to contemplate that from the time that Hashem said, "I am Hashem, your God", good and evil is in your hands.

LOOKING AHEAD

Re'eh, See, I place before you today blessing and curse.[5]

Why does the verse say "see" rather than "listen"?

Let us study the answer of the *Yalkut Shimoni.*

The *Yalkut* begins: Since Parashat Nitzavim says, "Life and death have I placed before you, blessing and curse,"[6] people might think they can take whichever path they choose. Therefore the verse continues: "And you shall choose life."

Why would anyone want to choose the path of curse and death?

The *Yalkut* answers with a parable of a person sitting at a fork in the road. Before him are two paths. He informs the passersby, "This path is smooth, but only for a few steps; it ends in thorns. That path is thorny; but after you go a few steps through the thorns, in the end it turns smooth." Similarly, Moshe said to the Jewish people: You see evildoers succeeding. But their success is only for a few days; in the end they will fall.

That is, the success of the wicked is short-lived, for Hashem has decreed that evil shall not endure. Ultimately they will meet their downfall in this world and the next.

The *Yalkut* continues: And you see *tzaddikim* who suffer in this

---

5. Devarim 11:26.
6. Devarim 30:19.

world. They suffer for two or three days, but ultimately they will rejoice, as it is written, "in order to afflict you and in order to test you, to do you good in your end."[7]

Thus the path of the *tzaddikim* is thorny at first — for their own benefit, since one mitzvah done with difficulty is worth more than a hundred without. How much did Rabbi Shimon bar Yohai gain from the distress of studying Torah in a cave for thirteen years! And Eliyahu HaNavi blessed a man that his house would be destroyed, meaning that he would have mischievous children who would wreck his house. Why didn't he bless him with quiet children? In order to multiply his merits as if he had raised a hundred children.

The *Yalkut* then quotes a few verses, which we will discuss.

"The end of a matter is good because of its beginning"[8] — because of the difficulties in the beginning. The initial difficulties attach a person to the mitzvoth, because we become attached to whom or what we invest in.

A rich couple had a pampered only child. When the boy grew up, the father insisted that he go out to work and stand on his own two feet. But the mother having pity on him, said, "Take these fifty dollars, show them to father and tell him you have gone to work."

The son did so, and when his father saw the money he took it and threw it into the fire, saying, "Go to work."

The mother tried giving the son double the amount, and then triple, but each time, the scene repeated itself. Finally, the son gave in and went to work at an entry-level job. When he brought his meager earnings home, the father was about to throw this money, too, into the fire. "Stop!" screamed the son. "Don't do it!"

"Now I know that you have really gone to work," said the

---

7. Devarim 8:16.
8. Kohelet 7:8.

father. "Because you worked for the money you are attached to it."

In a letter the prophet Yirmiyahu sent from Jerusalem to the exiles in Babylon he explained why the exile had to last seventy years and no less. "For I know the thoughts that I am thinking about you — the word of Hashem; thoughts of peace and not for evil, to give you an end and a hope."[9] Metzudot David comments: They went into exile so that their heart would be humbled, but this would be the reason to give them a good end and hope after they returned to their Land.

"Light is sown for the *tzaddik*, and joy for the upright of heart."[10] Indeed, toward the end of the seventy years, Hashem saved the Jewish people from Haman's decree of total annihilation. Then "the Jews had light and gladness and joy and honor,"[11] and we received the holiday of Purim with *mishloah manot, matanot la'evyonim*, and a mitzvah feast.

Accordingly, *re'eh*, "see," means "look ahead into the future." That is what Issachar did. "He saw that tranquility was good..., so he bent his shoulder to bear."[12] If he saw that tranquility was good, why didn't he sit back in an easy chair? Because he looked ahead and saw the tranquility at the end of the path; and he understood that to achieve it, he needed to toil now.

Interestingly, *re'eh* is in the singular, while the continuation is in the plural. This shows that Moshe is addressing each individual according to his own life challenges. One person has to battle laziness to rise for the morning prayers; another has to grapple with a tendency to anger. Each one has his own stumbling block. After he overcomes it, the path becomes smooth, in this world and the next.

---

9. Yirmiyahu 29:11.
10. Tehilim 97:11.
11. Esther 8:16.
12. Bereshit 49:15.

Re'eh, "See, I place before you today blessing and curse" — Look far ahead, and even today you will see that after the thorny part, the path becomes smooth, and that the thorns, too, are a blessing.

FIRE AND SNOW

Aser te'aser, You shall surely tithe [literally: Tithe, you shall tithe] the entire crop...."[13]

Midrash Tanhuma[14] expounds the double verb *Aser te'aser* in an enigmatic way.

> "She fears not snow for her household, for all her household is clothed in scarlet wool."[15] [The Jewish people do not fear Gehinnom because they are clothed in mitzvoth.]
>
> The judgment of wicked [Jews] in Gehinnom is twelve months, six months in heat, and six months in cold. At first Hashem brings them into the heat, and they say, "This is Hashem's Gehinnom." Afterward he takes them out into the snow, and they say, "This is Hashem's cold." At first they say, "*Heh,*" and in the end the say, "*Vay*"....
>
> "For all her household is clothed in scarlet," refers to the mitzvoth because the Hebrew word for scarlet is *shanim,* which can be read as *shenayim,* which means two. This refers to the mitzvoth that are performed in two parts, such as the two parts of circumcision;[16] *tzitzit* and *tefillin*; ...*patoah tiftah*[17] ("Open, you shall open your hand to [the poor]); *Aser te'aser.* Therefore Moshe warns the Jewish people, *Aser te'aser.*

---

13. Devarim 14:22.
14. *Ot* 13.
15. Mishlei 31:21.
16. *Milah* and *periah.*
17. Devarim 15:8.

The Gemara[18] adds that in Gehinnom, Jewish sinners weep and shed tears like a fountain, [indicating their remorse and repentance]. They accept Hashem's judgment and say, "Master of the world, fairly have You judged, acquitted, condemned, and ordained Gehinnom for the wicked."[19]

Shaarei Teshuvah[20] explains that although when a Jew repents, Hashem forgives, a stain of sin may remain on his soul. The laundering process that removes the stain consists of anguish at having transgressed Hashem's Will.

This is provided by Gehinnom. Six months of heat remove the pleasure of sin, and then six months of penetrating cold remove the last traces.

The first six months, they say, "*Heh.*" Why? With the letter *heh* (ה), say our Sages,[21] this world was created. The *heh* has a large opening at the bottom, to teach that if a person wishes to drop out of the framework of serving Hashem, he has freedom of choice to do so. During the first six months in Gehinnom, people regret having left the framework. During the last six months, they say, "*Vay,*" an expression of anguish for having sinned.

The Gemara continues: The fire of Gehinnom does not consume Jewish sinners, for they are filled with mitzvot like a pomegranate.[22]

Thus "She fears not snow for her household" — although they pass through the snow of Gehinnom, it is only to launder them; and then they go on to Gan Eden. "For all her household is clothed in [mitzvot] done in pairs" — they are full of mitzvot like a pomegranate, which is completely full, with no empty spaces.

---

18. *Eruvin* 19a.
19. Based on Tehilim 84:7.
20. Chapter 1.
21. *Menahot* 29b
22. See Shir HaShirim 4:3.

The same Gemara[23] teaches that wicked gentiles, in contrast, are always called sinners, and they do not repent even in Gehinnom.[24]

Our Sages[25] said that before Onkelos converted, he conjured up the spirit of Titus and asked him, "Who is most esteemed in the next world?"

"Israel," replied Titus.

"What about joining them?" asked Onkelos.

Titus replied, "Go attack them!"

Then Onkelos conjured up Bilaam's spirit and asked him, "Who is most esteemed in the next world?"

"Israel," replied Bilaam

"What about joining them?" asked Onkelos.

Bilaam replied, "Never seek their good!"

Titus and Bilaam also told Onkelos how terribly they were suffering in Gehinnom. These gentile sinners suffer, know the truth, and yet cannot purify their souls. For in the next world, a person has only what he brings with him from here. Jewish sinners are able to purify their souls through Gehinnom because in this world they regretted their sins.

When we arrive there, we will not want to be told, "Sorry, this stain cannot be removed." The solution is simple: Train ourselves to feel regret whenever we do something wrong. Then we will be able to complete our *teshuvah*[26] in the next world as a continuation of what we did here.

---

23. *Eruvin* 19a.
24. Based on Yeshayahu 66:24.
25. *Gittin* 56b.
26. Repentance.

PARASHAT

Shofetim

LEARNING FROM THE ANT

Judges and law enforcement agents shall you appoint in all your gates....[1]

The Midrash[2] here expounds on Shelomo HaMelech's words: "Go to the ant, O lazy one; see its ways and grow wise. Though she has no officer, law enforcer, or ruler, she prepares her bread in the summer and stores her food in the harvest time."[3]

Why did Shelomo HaMelech teach the lazy one from the ant?

Our Sages said: The ant's chambers has three levels. She does not store her food in the upper one because it might get wet from the rain, nor in the bottom one because of the dampness, but only in the middle one. She eats only one and a half kernels of wheat her entire life, yet in the summer she goes and gathers whatever she finds — wheat, oats, and lentils.

Rabbi Tanhuma said: Once three hundred measures of wheat were found in an ant's storage supply, so that should Hashem decree on her a long life, the food would be ready.

---

1. Devarim 16:18.
2. *Devarim Rabbah ot* 2.
3. Mishlei 6:6–8.

Therefore Shelomo HaMelech said, "Go to the ant, O lazy one; see its ways and grow wise" — you, too, prepare yourselves mitzvot in this world for the world to come.

And what did Shlomo mean by "see its ways and grow wise"? He meant see her proper conduct in fleeing from robbery. Said Rabbi Shimon ben Halafta: An ant once dropped a kernel of wheat. All the ants came and smelled it, but not one took it, until the ant who dropped it came and took it. See what wisdom she has, she refrains from robbery even without a law enforcer or ruler. All the more so you, for whom I have appointed judges and law enforcement agents, should refrain from robbery.

How does storing food in the middle level and refraining from robbery teach a lazy person?

We find a clue in the key words, "Prepare yourselves with mitzvot in this world for the world to come." How to do this we learn from the ant?

The quality of the mitzvah should be learned from the ant. The ant stores its food in the middle level so that it will stay fine and tasty for the winter. We, too, should do mitzvot in the best possible way so that they will arrive "fine and tasty" in the world to come. Doing mitzvoth in the best possible way means doing them because of Hashem's command; with joy; and with love. Thus in the blessing over a mitzvah, we say, "Who has sanctified us with His commandments [plural]" because each mitzvah has branches: intent, joy, and love.

The quantity of the mitzvah should also be learned from the ant. The ant gathers tremendous quantities; and we have come to this world to gather the most mitzvot possible, as *Mesilat Yesharim* says.[4]

A parable is given about the boss of a large plant who sent one

---

4. Chapter 1.

of his truck drivers to buy merchandise at the port. "Drive carefully!" the boss warned him.

The driver set out on the road. He drove very carefully to the port, and then turned around and, driving very carefully, returned.

"How was your trip?" asked the boss.

"I drove very carefully," replied the driver.

"Excellent," said the boss. "And where's the merchandise that you bought?"

"That slipped my mind," said the driver. "But I thought the main thing was to drive carefully."

Many of us think that the main thing in our trip through this world is to avoid sinning. Of course we mustn't sin; but the main thing is to "buy merchandise" — acquire mitzvot.

Thinking about life should also be learned from the ant. A thief may be nimble and quick, but he is lazy when it comes to thinking about life. He does not devote time to think about his deeds and why he has been given life.

What prevents us from stockpiling high-quality mitzvot, and thinking about what we are doing here? The evil inclination, or *yetzer, which* wages a continual war against us every day, all day, beginning the minute we open our eyes in the morning. Will we arise quickly? Will we hurry and prepare for Shaharit? And will we pray properly? The battle is on.

Our verse therefore says, "Judges and law enforcement agents shall you appoint in all your gates...." In the Hebrew, "you" and "your" are in the singular; the individual is being addressed. So our Sages understood this as an injunction to every individual to police his *yetzer*. Thus the Gemara[5] says: *Tzaddikim* are judged by the good inclination; evildoers, by the evil inclination.

---

5. *Berachot* 61b.

On the verse about the ant, the Midrash[6] says: In the world to come, the wicked will ask Hashem to let them repent. He will tell them, "Fools! *Olam hazeh*[7] resembles Erev Shabbat, and *olam haba*[8] resembles Shabbat. If a person does not prepare on Erev Shabbat, what will he eat on Shabbat? *Olam hazeh* resembles the land; *olam haba,* the sea. If he does not take provisions from land, what will he have at sea? *Olam hazeh* resembles sunny seasons; *olam haba,* rainy seasons. If he does not plow, sow, and harvest in the sunny seasons, what will he eat in the rainy seasons?

This medrash is referring to the three types of preparation of mitzvot in this world for the world to come:

The first is the quantity of mitzvot. To survive at sea, a person must fill his baggage with many items on land. Similarly, in order to live in the next world, we must fill our baggage with many mitzvot here.

The second is the quality of mitzvot. To enjoy delicacies on Shabbat, a person must prepare delicacies on Erev Shabbat. To enjoy the world to come, we must prepare quality mitzvot here. The quality of our *olam haba,* says *Mesilat Yesharim,*[9] depends on the quality of the mitzvot we do here.

The third, is that we must pray. A person who plows and sows must pray that rain will fall and that his crop will not be ruined by frost, insects, etc. Similarly, we must pray about our Torah and mitzvot. We must pray that we will remember what we learn and use it in our lives, and that our mitzvot will influence others.

6. *Yalkut Shimoni,* Mishlei, ch. 6.
7. This world.
8. The world to come.
9. Chapter 1.

APPOINTING A KING

When you come to the Land… and you will say, "I will appoint a king over myself, like all the nations that are around me," you shall surely appoint a king over yourself.…[10]

Says the Rambam:[11] The Jewish people were commanded to do three mitzvot when they entered the Land: Appoint a king, eradicate Amalek, and build the Temple.

If so, why was Shemuel HaNavi angry when the people asked him for a king?[12]

Says the Rambam:[13] Because they asked in a quarrelsome manner, and because they did not want a king in order to fulfill the mitzvah, but because they rejected Shemuel.

Why did they reject Shemuel who saved them from the Philistines with his prayers, and who judged them by Torah law?[14]

The Gemara[15] says: The elders of the generation, in fact, asked properly,[16] but the ignorant asked improperly.[17] The Sifri[18] says: They asked for a king in order to worship idols, as Hashem told Shemuel, "It is not you whom they have rejected, but Me whom they have rejected from reigning over them.… They forsook Me and worshiped the gods of others."[19]

Perhaps we can explain that the ignorant didn't want to actually worship idols, rather, they wanted a king who would judge them

---

10. Devarim 17:14–15.
11. *Hilchot Melachim* 1:1.
12. See Shemuel 1, ch. 8.
13. *Hilchot Melachim* 1:2.
14. See Shemuel 1 ch. 7
15. *Sanhedrin* 20b.
16. See Shemuel 1 8:4.
17. See Shemuel 1 8:20.
18. Cited by Radak.
19. Shemuel 1 8:7–8.

like all the nations. As Rashi says:[20] We are commanded to bring our litigation before *bet din,* which judges in accordance with Torah law. One who goes to a court that does not judge by Torah law is desecrating Hashem's Name and honoring the gods of the gentiles.

They rejected Torah law, which is strikingly different from gentile law. For instance, Torah law requires two witnesses, neither of whom may be a woman or the litigant's relative or enemy. Circumstantial evidence is not accepted. However, the Rambam[21] says, a king and even a Jewish king, if necessary to safeguard society, may give the death penalty on the basis of one witness and without warning. This is not meant to supplant *bet din,*[22] rather he does so under exceptional circumstances.

This explains why Sifri says that the people asked for a king in order to worship idols. Since the king can judge in ways that are outside of Torah law, one who desires the king for this reason, is like honoring the gods of the gentiles.

The mitzvah of having a king is not to supplant Torah law, rather to enforce it.

In fact, the Jewish king must have an extra attachment to Torah. Every Jew must cleave to Torah, but the king must cleave to it even more, as the Rambam says:[23] The king is commanded to keep a Sefer Torah with him at all times, as it is written, "It shall be with him, and he shall read in it all the days of his life."[24]

The Rambam[25] also states the reason for the king's extra attachment to Torah:

---

20. On Shemot 21:1, citing Tanhuma.
21. *Hilchot Melachim* 3:10.
22. Court.
23. *Hilchot Melachim* 3:1.
24. Devarim 17:19.
25. *Hilchot Melachim,* end of 3:5.

The Torah is particular that the king's heart not move away from the Torah, as it is written, "His heart shall not move away."[26] For his heart is the heart of the entire community of Israel. Therefore Scripture attaches him to the Torah more than the rest of the people, as it is written, "all the days of his life."

What is the significance of the king being the nation's heart? The heart's function is to pump life-giving blood to all members of the body. Similarly, the king's function is to pump life-giving Torah to all members of the nation.

Until Mashiah reigns, our discussion of the king is theoretical. But Rashi's stern warning against going to non-Jewish or secular courts applies to us today.

EGLAH ARUFAH

If a corpse is found... fallen in the field [and] it was not known who smote him, your elders and judges shall go out.... and measure the distance between the victim and the surrounding cities.[27] [The closest city must bring a calf which is killed after the elders declare that they are not responsible for shedding this blood.]

If innocent blood has been shed in our Holy Land, the entire nation must be shaken up. Five judges from the Great Sanhedrin in Jerusalem — and (according to one opinion) even the king and the Kohen Gadol — come to measure the distance between the victim and the surrounding cities.

Then the procedure of the *eglah arufah* is carried out, as if to say: We do not forgive the murderer. We have not yet found him, but when we do, we will execute him, even fifty years from now.

---

26. Devarim 17:17.
27. Devarim 21:1–2.

Targum Yonatan says that worms would travel from the slain calf to the murderer, enabling them to catch him.

The city's court of twenty-three judges and its Kohanim come and the judges say, "Our hands did not shed this blood and our eyes did not see."[28] Although no one suspects them of murder, their declaration means: We had no part in allowing the victim to leave the city alone without food or escort.[29] The Kohanim say, "Atone for Your people Israel...."[30]

Atonement is necessary because since a murder took place near the city there must have been an accusation against the city[31] or perhaps the townspeople committed a similar sin.[32] The victim might have passed through, and no one paid attention to him, so he fell into despair and could not defend himself. The city could have established a *hesed*[33] organization to help wayfarers.[34]

Why do the city's leaders — its judges and Kohanim —say these words? Because the guilt of the people is blamed on their leaders who should have rebuked them and directed them to the path of righteousness.[35]

Finally, the Kli Yakar asks: Why is the *eglah arufah* inserted among four passages dealing with war?

We might answer that when the Torah commands us to wage war against our enemies, we must do so without pity.[36] At the same time, the *eglah arufah* comes to teach us how seriously the Torah takes human life.

---

28. Devarim 21:6–7.
29. Rashi.
30. Devarim 21:8.
31. Zohar, Vayera 113.
32. Ibn Ezra, cited also by Ramban.
33. Kindness.
34. *Sotah* 45b.
35. See Rashi, Devarim 1:13.
36. See Rashi, Devarim 20:12.

PARASHAT

Ki Tetzei

RELEASING THE CAPTIVE

When you go out to war against your enemies... and you see among
the captives a beautiful woman (*yefat toar*)... she shall weep for her
father and her mother for a full month.[1]

Says the Zohar: The *yefat toar* alludes to the soul, and the
month mentioned here alludes to the month of Elul.

Throughout the year, when people are asleep, so to speak, the
soul is held captive by the evil inclination of lusts, laziness, and
other bad character traits. But when Elul comes, the Selihot prayers
and shofar blasts wake them up; and the weeping helps release their
souls from captivity.

The *Ohr HaHayyim* explains that when the verse says the soul
weeps "for her father and her mother," "her father" alludes to
Hashem, and, "her mother," alludes to the community of Israel.

We can understand how weeping helps the soul return to
"her father" — Hashem. But what is meant by weeping for "her
mother" — the community of Israel?

We may answer in light of a parable that the Midrash[2] uses to
explain why Hashem did not reveal the reward for each mitzvah.

---

1. Devarim 21:10–13.
2. Devarim Rabbah, *ot* 2.

A king instructed his servants to hoe under the trees of his orchard. When the servants finished working, he paid each one a different amount, based on the tree under which he had hoed.

"Why didn't you tell us the payment for each tree?" they asked.

"If I had told you," he replied, "what would have become of my orchard?"

The orchard is the community of Israel, as in "My Beloved has descended to His garden."[3] Every mitzvah done by a Jew contributes to the beauty and completeness of the community of Israel, which is built up over the generations. Each individual has his part to contribute, without which the orchard would be incomplete.

On Rosh HaShannah, not only is each individual judged separately.[4] There is also a judgment of everyone at once,[5] to determine whether the individual has done his part to complete the orchard.

In preparation, the soul weeps in Elul "for her father and her mother" — to return and cleave to Hashem; and to fix any lack in contributing to the community of Israel.

*   *   *

One important aspect of weeping to Hashem, is regretting sins that the person has decided "this prohibition is not for me."

The Hafetz Hayyim[6] asks: How could the Spies say, "We cannot ascend against that nation because it is too strong for us"?[7] Hadn't they seen Hashem smite Egypt with the Ten Plagues and drown its army in the sea?

He answers: They thought that after the sin of the golden calf,

---

3. Shir HaShirim 6:2.
4. *Kivnei maron.*
5. *Biskirah ahat.*
6. Commentary on the Parshiot, in the back of *Shemirat HaLashon.*
7. Bamidbar 13:31.

they were no longer righteous enough for Hashem to miraculously vanquish their enemies. Although they had repented completely, for when Moshe went up to heaven to pray that Hashem forgive them, they had wept and fasted, they underestimated the power of repentance.

Calev contradicted the spies and said, "We shall surely ascend and conquer it."[8] He then told them, "But do not rebel against Hashem!"[9]

They claimed they were unable to conquer the land, why is this considered a rebellion?

When Hashem gives a command and people say, "We can't; it's too hard for us; we aren't *tzaddikim*" — that is rebellion.

Similarly, Shaarei Teshuvah[10] says: Some people are not careful to avoid a particular sin. Our Sages call them "apostates in one matter." This is a very grave thing, for if a servant tells his master, "I'll do everything you say except for one thing," he is casting off his master's yoke.

Thus if a person says, "Mitzvah X is hard for me to fulfill; it's not for me because I'm not a *tzaddik*," he is rebelling against Hashem.

Moreover, since he regards this sin as permitted, he has no pangs of conscience and no regret. If so, he will not be cleansed even in the world to come, for there can be no repentance that has not begun here.

In Elul, "she shall weep for her father." Elul is the time to for us to ask ourselves, "Are there commands of Hashem that I take lightly?" It's the time to undo our rebellion and disconnect from bad habits. It's the time to say, "I'm sorry and I want to change and leave captivity.

---

8. Bamidbar 13:30.
9. Bamidbar 14:9.
10. 1:6.

The regret we feel in this world will help us enormously in the world to come.

EFFECTIVE PARENTING

If a man has a wayward, rebellious son (*ben sorer umoreh*), who does not heed the voice of his father and the voice of his mother....[11]

Says the Gemara:[12] Can it be that because he ate a measure of meat and drank a measure of wine his father and mother take him out to be stoned? Rather, there never was and never will be such a case. The law of *ben sorer umoreh* was only taught for us to expound and receive reward.

Among the criteria that prevent the law from being imposed, continues the Gemara, is that his father and mother must have the same voice, since they must tell the court, "He does not heed our voice."[13]

Then the Gemara states: Just as their voice must be the same, so too, must their appearance and height be the same.

What is the logic in all this?

We might answer as follows.

The parents are, in effect, telling the court, "It is not our fault that he is wayward and rebellious since we gave him a proper upbringing." But what is a proper upbringing? One in which the parents' voice, appearance, and height are equal, as we will explain.

The "voice of his father" should be tough, and "the voice of his mother" gentle, but both must say the same thing. If they contradict each other — if the father says, "Get up for Shaharit," and the

---

11. Devarim 22:18.
12. *Sanhedrin* 71a.
13. Devarim 21:20.

mother says, "He's tired; let him sleep" — then the parents are at fault for what became of him.

Parents must deliver the same message not only verbally, but with their facial expressions as well. Both must be visibly shaken when he lies or steals and show disapproval at his misdeeds.

When the sages say they must have the same height, it means that the parents must live in harmony. If one looks down on the other, they are at fault in his upbringing. As the Gemara[14] says: If your wife is short, bend over and whisper to her. That is, if the wife is on a lower lever that her husband, he should lower himself to speak with her. They must sort things out between them privately and present a united front to their children.

It is said that a home is like a yeshiva. The father is like the rosh yeshiva for he is in charge of the children's Torah study. The mother is like the mashgiah, as it says in *Eshet Hayyil,* "She watches over the ways of her house."[15] Her function is to teach *derech eretz*[16] and good *midot,*[17] and to impart a desire for studying Torah and *mussar.*[18]

Rashi[19] explains *moreh* — rebellious — to mean he rebels against his father's words. Accordingly, we may say that *sorer* — *wayward,* which Rashi explains to mean turning from the right path, refers to what his mother taught him.

Nevertheless, a father should not act as a rosh yeshiva all the time. Our Sages relate that a man once came to Rabbi Yehudah HaNassi with a will from his deceased father saying that he leaves his possessions to his son on condition that he acts foolish.

14. *Bava Metzia* 59a.
15. Mishlei 31:27.
16. Proper conduct.
17. Character traits.
18. The study of self-improvement.
19. Devarim 21:18.

Puzzled, Rabbi Yehudah HaNassi went to consult Rabbi Yehoshua ben Korhah.

When they approached his house, they saw through the window a strange sight. The great Sage was on all fours, running after his little child and making baby sounds. They decided it would not be tactful to go in just then.

When they came later and presented the question, he replied, "It's a pity you did not come earlier — you would have seen the meaning of this with your own eyes!"

That is, a father must come down to his child's world and guide him from there.

Rav Shach *zt"l* said: Why did the Steipler's *zt"l* children turn out so well? Because after the Shabbat meal, he did not run to open a Gemara, but stayed with them, listened to them, and took an interest in their world.

JUDGED FOR HIS END

And all Israel shall hear and shall fear.[20]

The Gemara[21] teaches: The *ben sorer umoreh*[22] is executed because of what he will end up doing. To pay for his overindulgence in meat and wine, he will use up his father's money and then he will become a highway robber. The Torah therefore says: Let him die innocent and not die guilty.

But a person is judged according to his present state, and not according to his future one! Our Sages[23] learn this from the fact

---

20. Devarim 21:21.
21. *Sanhedrin* 71a.
22. Wayward, rebellious son.
23. *Rosh HaShannah* 16b.

that Hashem heard Yishmael's prayer "in his present state"[24] and saved him from dying of thirst.

We may explain in light of a story from the days of the Cantonist decree in Czarist Russia, when young Jewish children were kidnapped and forced to serve in the army for twenty-five years. A widow whose only son was taken brought a note to the Rebbe of Tchernobel with a shocking request. She asked him to pray that her son would die.

She was summoned and asked for an explanation. "My son has been abducted into the army," she said. "I won't see him again in this world. If he dies now, at least I'll see him in the world to come. But if he stays in the army for twenty-five years, I won't see him there, either."

The Rebbe surely did not pray that the child would die. Instead, he shook the heavens praying that Hashem would return the child to his mother, and he sent his Hassidim to try to release him.

Accordingly, we may explain that the parents of the *ben sorer umoreh* say to the court: Our son is going in a direction where he will turn into a robber and killer, and then we will not see him either in this world or the next. We ask and pray that he die now, so that at least we will see him in the world to come.

"And all Israel shall hear and shall fear" — the people will be shocked by the parents' request that their son be killed, and they will help them return the son to the right path.

The Gemara[25] says: "A rebellious child in a person's house is more painful than the War of Gog and Magog." Against the frightening attack by Gog and Magog, all of Israel will fight and will win. The parents who don't know what to do with their rebellious

---

24. Bereshit 21:17.
25. *Berachot* 7a.

child are caught in a painful, lonely struggle. But if all of Israel help them solve the problem, they will succeed.

*   *   *

Alternatively, we might say that usually a person is judged by how he will end up, as in the case of the *ben sorer umoreh,* however, Yishmael was judged "in his present state" because he and his mother, Hagar, prayed from a broken heart.

We can learn the power of prayer to change a decree, from Leah, about whom it was decreed that she marry the wicked Esav. But her tearful prayers turned over the decree and she married Yaakov Avinu.

Similiarly, when Esav discovered that Yaakov had taken the blessings, he asked Yitzhak Avinu, "Have you not reserved a blessing for me?"[26] Yitzhak replied "And for you, then, what can I do, my son?"[27] — there is no blessing left. Then "Esav raised his voice and wept"[28] — and suddenly, Yitzhak had blessings to give him! Such is the power of tears.

On Rosh HaShannah and Yom Kippur, Hashem judges us according to our broken-heartedness now, which is why we read the Parashah of Yishmael on Rosh HaShannah.

Shaarei Teshuvah[29] says that part of *teshuvah* is to pray that our sins be atoned. Besides removing our sins, there is an additional benefit in doing *teshuva.* For our Sages[30] said, "A sin extinguishes a mitzvah" [that is, the mitzvah does not have great merit]. When our sins are atoned, the light of our mitzvot is restored.

---

26. Bereshit 27:36.
27. Bereshit 27:37.
28. Bereshit 27:38.
29. 1:41.
30. *Sotah* 21a.

Similarly, the Rambam[31] said: How wonderful is *teshuvah*! Yesterday when the person did mitzvot, they were ripped up in his face, but now he does mitzvot and they are accepted with pleasantness and joy.

May our return to Hashem on Rosh HaShannah, re-light our mitzvot and tip the scales in favor of the entire Jewish people.

AMALEK

> Remember what Amalek did to you... that he happened upon you (*karecha*) on the way.... He did not fear God.[32]

Rashi explains the word *karecha* as chance (*mikreh*), coldness (*kor*), and impurity (*keri*). He says: The nations were afraid to fight Israel until Amalek came and showed the way to others. The matter may be likened to a bath of boiling water that no one could enter. One scoundrel (*beli'al*) came and jumped in. Although he himself was burned, he made it appear cool to others.

The splitting of the sea had cast fear of the Jewish people upon all the nations, as it is written, "Peoples heard and were agitated, terror gripped Philistia's inhabitants, Edom's chieftains were frightened...."[33] Came Amalek and proclaimed, "It was all chance," much as apostates today proclaim that it was a natural event. Amalek even convinced other nations to join in its attack against Israel, as it is written, "Yehoshua weakened Amalek and his people by the sword's blade."[34] "His people," says the Seforno, refers to other nations that joined Amalek.

Amalek could not penetrate the protective cover of the Clouds

---

31. Hilchot Teshuvah 7:7.
32. Devarim 25:17–18.
33. Shemot 15:14–15.
34. Shemot 17:13.

of Glory. He attacked members of the Tribe of Dan who had been expelled because of their sins, and other Jews whom he called to come out and buy his wares. Amalek was only able to defile and kill these Jews. He also cut their circumcisions, threw them heavenward, and said, "This is what You have chosen? Take them!"[35]

Amalek "did not fear God"[36] — he recognized Hashem but deliberately rebelled against Him. Thus Rashi calls Amalek *beli'al*, literally: "without a yoke,"[37] like his ancestor Esav, who recognized Hashem but denied Him.

Amalek is the power of evil in the world, the power that wants to drive us off the right path. To this day, he cools off our fear of heaven and makes us view Hashem's wonders and supervision as chance

Why did Hashem allow Amalek to attack Israel?

Rashi[38] answers with a parable.

A father carried his son on his shoulder and set out on the road. Along the way, the son would ask his father for things, and his father would give them to him. After a while, they encountered someone, and the son asked him, "Have you seen Father?"

"You don't know where I am?!" said the father. He threw the son down, and a dog came and bit him.

The dog, of course, is Amalek. But what is meant by "Have you seen Father?"

The father gave the son everything, and the son took the father's kindness for granted.

The little Amalek within us causes us to see everything as chance rather than as the hand of Hashem. And then, measure for measure, Amalek attacks from without.

---

35. See Rashi, Devarim 25:18; *Tanhuma* 10.
36. Devarim 25:18.
37. *Beli ol.*
38. Shemot 17:8.

Hovot HaLevavot[39] observes that people forget to gratefully thank Hashem for the wonderful favors He showers upon them daily — because they are used to them and take them for granted.

So on Rosh HaShannah and Yom Kippur, we say in *Avinu malkenu,* "Our Father, our King, we have no king but You." You are our Father, Who showers us with good all year long. We have not forgotten You. Be to us like a father who always loves his son, even if he rebels!

The little Amalek within also cools our fear of Hashem and makes us quickly forget any spiritual awakening that we might have.

In Parashat Beshalah, which describes the war against Amalek, we read that "when Moshe raised his hand, Israel was stronger."[40] The Ramban explains that Moshe in effect led the Jews in prayer. When they saw him kneel, they knelt; when he fell on his face, they fell on their faces; when he spread his hands heavenward, they spread their hands heavenward.

But the verse continues: "and when he lowered his hand. Amalek was stronger." How did that happen, when they had just subjugated their hearts to Hashem, and He had accepted their prayers?

We may explain in light of the Shaarei Teshuvah's[41] teaching: If a person does not arouse himself, how will *mussar* help? For although it enters his heart the day he hears it, the *yetzer hara* will make him forget it. So when he hears *mussar,* he must arouse himself, take the words to heart, ponder them, add his own thoughts, and rebuke himself.

Accordingly, the moment the Jews stopped subjugating their

---

39. Introduction to *Shaar HaBehinah.*
40. Shemot 17:11.
41. *Shaar* 2, *ot* 26.

hearts to Hashem and praying, the *yetzer hara* came to cool their spiritual awakening.

What is the solution? Repetition and review. Thus Rabbi Yisrael Salanter was heard repeating a line of rebuke from a Mishnah half a night.

This explains why the shofar is blown repeatedly on Rosh HaShannah — to confuse Satan (also known as the *yetzer hara*) and to strengthen the impression on us. For the shofar blasts are a type of *mussar,* as the Rambam says:[42]

> Although the blowing of shofar is a decree of the Torah, there is a hint in it: Wake up, you sleepers, from your sleep.... Examine your deeds, do *teshuvah*, and remember your Creator!

---

42. *Hilchot Teshuvah* 3:4.

PARASHAT
Ki Tavo

BIKURIM[1]

You shall take of the first (*reshit*) of every fruit....[2] [bring it to the Beit Hamikdash, and give it to the Kohen after making a declaration thanking Hashem for all his kindness beginning from when Lavan tried to kill Yaakov, including the Exodus from Egypt, until He brought us into the land.]

Our Sages[3] taught: "*Be-reshit* — for the sake of the first [fruits] — Hashem created heaven and earth."[4]

What is so special about *bikurim*?

To answer this question, let us study the mitzvah.

Rashi says that when one brings *bikurim* to the Temple, he must raise his voice as he thanks Hashem for saving Yaakov Avinu from Lavan, for redeeming the Jewish people from Egypt, for bringing them to the Land of Israel, as well as for his crop. [5]

Why does this require raising his voice?

This can be compared to a rich man who told his relative, "Bring a large chest, and I will put money into it for you." When

---

1. First fruits.
2. Devarim 26:2.
3. *Bereshit Rabbah*, Bereshit 5.
4. Bereshit 1:1.
5. Devarim 26:5.

he puts in the first bill, the recipient says, "Thank you." When the second bill is put in, the recipient says, "Thank you very much." With each additional bill, the recipient expresses his gratitude with more excitement, until he is calling out loudly.

Similarly, when Yitro heard about all the miracles that occurred during the redemption from Egypt, he was moved to the point that, *Vayihad Yitro* — "Yitro rejoiced greatly over all the good that Hashem had done for Israel."[6] He then added, *"Baruch Hashem,* blessed is Hashem."[7] The word *berachah,* "blessing," actually means increase, multiplication, and abundance. Since the many miracles were presented to him at once, he said, *Baruch Hashem.*

Accordingly, when one replies, *"Baruch Hashem"* to the question "How are you?" besides thanking Hashem that he feels well today, he should see in his mind's eye all of the good Hashem has bestowed upon him.

In connection with *bikurim,* the Torah says, "You shall rejoice with all the good that Hashem, your God, has given you and your household."[8] Rashi explains this to mean: You should not be *kefui tovah,* ungrateful.

Literally, *kefui tovah* means "covering the good," for the word *kofeh* means to cover, as used by our Sages when they said, "If a person finds hametz on Pesach he must cover (*kofeh*) it with a vessel so that it will not be seen. Rashi is saying: Don't cover and forget all the favors that Hashem has done for you. Recognize them so that you will be happy.

Hashem created the world in order to bestow good on men. Or, as the Midrash says, the world was created for *bikurim,* for this mitzvah causes a person to "rejoice with all the good."

---

6. Shemot 18:9.
7. Shemot 18:10.
8. Devarim 26:11.

Indeed, *bikurim* were brought with great excitement and rejoicing. The Mishnah[9] relates that people came from many towns and camped overnight in the plaza of a city. In the morning, they sang chapters of Tehilim to the accompaniment of musical instruments, and leading an ox with gold-plated horns for a sacrifice, they approached Jerusalem, where they were greeted and escorted to the Temple Mount.

Says the Hovot HaLevavot:[10] Four things arouse a person to *teshuvah:* recognizing the good that Hashem does for him, hearing rebuke and studying *mussar,* seeing others suffer, and suffering himself. The best way of arousal is the first one; to return to Hashem because of the good that He does for us.

With this we can explain the statement in our Parashah that curses come "because you did not serve Hashem, your God, amid gladness and goodness of heart when everything was abundant."[11] That is, had you awakened to *teshuvah* from the good that Hashem gave you, you would not have needed the curses to awaken you.

Let us return to the verse, *"Ve'anita — and you shall answer and say — [Lavan,] the Aramite tried to destroy [Yaakov] my father...* We have already quoted Rashi who translates *Ve'anita* to mean "you shall call out loudly." Targum renders it as: "You shall return" — that is, do *teshuvah.* However, the simple translation is, "you shall answer." Who asked a question?

Based on the Hovot HaLevavot, we might explain that the *bikurim,* so to speak, are asking the one who brought them: What is your response to the kindness that Hashem is bestowing on you?

Similarly, a verse in our Parashah says: "All these blessings

---

9. *Masechet Bikurim.*
10. *Shaar HaTeshuvah,* ch. 6.
11. Devarim 28:47.

will come upon you, *vehisigucha* - and they will overtake you."[12] The Kotzker Rebbe *zt"l* said that we can also translate *vehisigucha* to mean, "and they will question you," as in the Ravad's *hasagot,* "questions," on the Rambam. For once all these blessings come upon you, they question you: Why aren't your deeds in keeping with your blessings?

Ve'anita, you shall answer and call out, "Father, I understand! I know that I must rejoice in Your kindness and return to You."

Thus the world was created for *bikurim* — so that man would recognize his Creator and joyfully thank Him.

---

12. Devarim 28:2.

PARASHAT

Nitzavim

WITHIN OUR GRASP

For this mitzvah that I command you today — it is not hidden from you and it is not distant. It is not in heaven... and it is not across the sea... Rather, the matter is very near to you, in your mouth and your heart, to do it.[1]

Which mitzvah is being discussed here?

According to Rashi, the mitzvah is Torah study.

Thus the passage means: Let a person not say that understanding Torah is "in heaven" — beyond his abilities — or "across the sea" — too vast for anyone to know. Midrash Rabbah teaches that Hashem asks of a person only what he is capable of: "in your mouth" — the amount that you are able to study (studying is meant to be done aloud, with the mouth); and "in your heart" — as much you are able to understand (the heart is considered the seat of understanding).

According to Ramban, the mitzvah is *teshuvah*. Repentance is "in your mouth" — you must verbally confess your sins; and you must also return to Hashem "in your heart."

Teshuvah is not "in heaven" or "across the sea" — it is not

---

1. Devarim 30:11–14.

beyond reach. If a person begins to repent, Hashem will help him succeed. The Shaarei Teshuvah[2] states: Hashem will help those who wish to repent if they cannot do it themselves, and He will give them a new spirit of purity to acquire love of Him, as it is written [in our Parashah], "You will return unto Hashem, your God, and heed His voice, according to all that I command you today, you and your children, with all your heart and with all your soul."[3]

In Parashat Ekev, we find: "You shall circumcise the foreskin of your heart."[4] Whereas in our Parashah, we find: "And Hashem, your God, will circumcise the foreskin of your heart."[5] This is not a contradiction, for if you just begin the process, Hashem will continue.

Rav Yitzhak Zilberstein *shlita*, in *Alenu Leshabeah* relates an instance of Hashem's help in doing *teshuvah* in our times. A non-observant Israeli had a religious neighbor who constantly urged him to start keeping mitzvot, but without success. One day this Israeli flew to Europe searching for his family roots. He entered the old synagogue in his grandfather's hometown and opening a Sukot *mahzor* he was overcome with emotion at the sight of his grandfather's name. Turning the pages, he found a *hadas*[6] leaf. That broke him completely, and on the spot he decided to keep Torah and mitzvot.

Hashem had helped — but what did the person himself contribute first?

Apparently, allowing his neighbor to speak to him was sufficient. Then, as soon as his heart opened, the words he had heard

---

2. *Shaar* 1, *ot* 1.
3. Devarim 30:2.
4. Devarim 10:16.
5. Devarim 30:6.
6. Myrtle, taken on Sukot with the *lulav* and *etrog*.

were able to enter. As a Torah scholar explained the verse, "These words, which I command you today, shall be upon your heart"[7] — place them upon your heart so that when your heart opens, they will enter.

*   *   *

What goes on in our heart is a key part of *teshuvah*. The *Mesilat Yesharim*[8] explains that when we totally regret a sin and grieve over it, Hashem considers the uprooting of our will as the uprooting of the deed and forgives us. Through this, "Your iniquity has been removed, and your sin will be atoned."[9]

This explains why we begin Yom Kippur with the excitement of *Kol Nidrei*. This prayer is the basis of all that we do on Yom Kippur. In *Kol Nidrei,* we ask that our regret of a vow go back to the time we made it and undo the vow. When we repent, we ask that our regret of our sin go back to the time we committed it and undo the sin.

In light of this, we may explain a line in *Avinu Malkenu*: "Our Father, our King, inscribe us in the book of merits." This is a puzzling request. For if we have merits, obviously Hashem will inscribe us. And if we don't, what can He inscribe?

Some explain that we are asking Hashem to give us opportunities to do mitzvot — for instance, by sending us a person who needs our help.

The Hafetz Hayyim[10] explains that we are speaking of mitzvot that we did out of self-interest rather than for Hashem. Such mitzvot have no place in the book of merits. But we ask Hashem, in

---

7. Devarim 6:6.
8. Chapter 4.
9. Yeshayahu 6:7.
10. Behukotai, p. 183, *Maasai LaMelech.*

His great kindness, to judge us favorably and inscribe even these.

We can understand this in light of the *Mesilat Yesharim*'s principle that Hashem considers uprooting the will as uprooting the deed. Here, too, we regret and grieve that the intentions behind these mitzvot were wrong, and we pray that Hashem will uproot those intentions and inscribe these mitzvot in the book of merits.

In Selihot we pray for both things. "May the Merciful One think well of us" — may He consider our mitzvot as having the right intention behind them. And "May the Merciful One give us the privilege of fulfilling more mitzvot."

PARASHAT

Vayelech

WHEN HASHEM'S FACE IS CONCEALED

My anger will flare against them on that day, and I will forsake them; and I will conceal My face from them, and they will become prey.... And I will surely conceal (*haster astir*) My face on that day because of all the evil that they did....[1]

Says the Gemara:[2] Whoever is not included in the decree of *hester panim*, "concealment of [Hashem's] face," or in the decree of, "they will become prey" is not one of them, [i.e. he is not part of the Jewish people.]

Rashi and Rabbenu Hananel both explain that the decree of "concealment of Hashem's face" means that their prayers are not answered. They explain the decree of, "becoming prey," means being plundered by idolaters.

The Gemara continues: The Sages pointed to Rava, as if to say, that he did not seem to be in either situation. That is, Hashem answered all His prayers; and idolaters did not touch his great wealth.

He replied, "I secretly send bribes to King Shevur [the Persian king who ruled over Babylon.]"

After that, Shevur's messengers came and robbed him.

---

1. Devarim 31:17–18.
2. *Hagigah* 5a.

111

This episode is puzzling. How dare the Sages imply that Rava, the great rosh yeshiva who appears on almost every page of the Gemara, was not of the Jewish people?

We might explain as follows. The verse is describing what happens when the Jewish people stray from Hashem. However, they did not expect these consequences to affect the generation's *tzaddikim*. Therefore they said that these decrees did not affect Rava. But, in fact, they did— because the *tzaddikim* are tied to the people.

Thus our Sages[3] relate that from when the generation of the desert fell into disfavor with Hashem as a result of the sin of the Spies, until the whole generation died out, Hashem spoke to Moshe Rabbenu without the usual affection.

If the people were distanced from Hashem, so was Moshe — because he tied himself to them.

Similarly, the Sages told Rava that he was not sufficiently tied to the Jewish people.

Rava replied that things were not as they appeared. He secretly sent bribes to the Persian king, and his prayer that he not suffer this monetary loss was not accepted.

Nevertheless, because it appeared to others as if he were not in *hester panim,* the king's messengers came and robbed him to show that indeed he was include in the verse "they will become prey."

Painful as *hester panim* is, it brings wonderful benefit if we respond correctly. How so?

The Gemara[4] states: If a person sees that his prayers are not answered, he should go back and pray again, as it is written, "Hope to Hashem; strengthen yourself, and he will give your heart courage; and hope [again] to Hashem."[5]

---

3. *Ta'anit* 30b; Rashi, Devarim 2:16.
4. *Berachot* 32b.
5. Tehilim 27:14.

How long should a person go on praying? Look at Yitzhak Avinu and his wife, Rivkah. It took them many, many years of praying for a child before Hashem answered them. For Hashem desires such heartfelt prayers. *Bitahon*[6] and extensive prayer purify, elevate, and sanctify a person's soul.

Our Sages[7] also said: Where is a hint to Esther found in the Torah? In the words "I will surely conceal (*haster astir*) My face."

This implies that there was *hester panim* in the time of Mordechai and Esther; Hashem did not answer their prayers. Rather than give up, the Jews fasted and prayed for three days straight. The happy result was that Hashem reversed Haman's decree of genocide and gave us the joyous holiday of Purim.

---

6. Trust.
7. *Hulin* 139b.

PARASHAT

Haazinu

HEAVEN AND EARTH

Give ear, heavens, and I will speak; and let the earth hear the words of my mouth. May my rebuke drop like the rain; may my utterance flow like the dew; like storm winds upon vegetation and like raindrops upon grass.[1]

Rashi comments that Moshe Rabbenu called upon the heavens and the earth to be enduring witnesses in case the Jewish people ever deny their acceptance of the covenant.

Note that Rashi does not speak of the Torah, but of the covenant. This refers to the covenant of mutual responsibility mentioned in Parashat Nitzavim — being guarantors (*arevim*) for one another's mitzvah observance.[2]

We can understand why people would deny their acceptance of this covenant, for as Hovot HaLevavot observes, it is very hard to fulfill the mitzvah of rebuking others.

Here Moshe suggests four ways of fulfilling the covenant of mutual responsibility. These are compared to rain, dew, storm winds, and heaven and earth.

---

1. Devarim 32:1–2.
2. See Rashi, Devarim 29:28.

"May my rebuke drop like the rain." Some people have a talent for rebuking; their words are like rainfall that makes the earth yield produce. They should use this talent.

"May my utterance flow like the dew," which makes produce grow although it itself is barely noticeable. Similarly, a person can influence others quietly, through his own proper conduct. One Jew related that he became observant because he saw a religious youth turn his face away from an improper sight.

"Like storm winds upon vegetation." Rashi comments: Just as these winds strengthen vegetation and make it grow, so do words of Torah make their learners grow.

And just as the world cannot exist without the winds, so it cannot exist without the Torah.

Says *Tanna d'Vei Eliyahu Zuta*:[3] The Jewish people will not be redeemed through suffering, subjugation, or poverty, but through ten people sitting together and learning each with his study partner, with their voices being heard. In other words, Kollelim will be opened in every city, and the "wind" of the Torah will blow and revive Jews everywhere. Today we see this happening throughout the world; may it expand and increase!

Finally, the Torah upbringing that we give our children will have an impact. Moshe calls out to all Jews: "Give ear, heavens…, and let the earth hear" — homiletically: Give ear to the heavens and listen to the earth! Hear and see what children are like when they are raised in the way of Torah, which comes from heaven — how much *derech eretz* they have, how pure they are, how much *nahat*[4] they bring their parents. Then hear and see what children are like when they are raised in the ways of earthliness and

---

3. Chapter 14, cited in Hafetz Hayyim on the Torah, Parashat Bo, p. 101a.
4. Satisfaction.

materialism, disconnected from Torah. See the great difference between the two, and let this bear witness to the truth.

Thus we have various ways of fulfilling our responsibility as guarantors, to which we are bound by covenant.

The Hafetz Hayyim[5] pointed out that in *Avinu Malkenu,* we pray, "Our Father, our King, forgive and pardon all our iniquities," and also, "Our Father, our King, erase, in Your abundant compassion, all the records of our debts." What "debts" — unfulfilled obligations to Hashem — remain after He pardons all our iniquities?

The sins of others, for which we, as guarantor, are responsible.

Before making this request, we must do our best to fulfill our duties as guarantors — by giving rebuke, or else by setting an example, learning Torah and supporting its study, and giving our children a fine Torah upbringing.

---

5. Parashat Behukotai, in *Maasai LaMelech*.

PARASHAT

VeZot HaBerachah

BLESSINGS AND KINDNESS

And this is the blessing that Moshe, the man of God, bestowed upon the Children of Israel before his death.[1]

Says Rashi: "Before his death" — close to his death, for if not now, when?

From here we understand that had it been possible, Moshe would have delayed giving the blessing even longer. Why? Wouldn't sooner have been better?

My grandson Michael answered that the blessing would be more effective the later it was given, for two reasons. The longer the *tzaddik* lives, the higher he ascends to levels of sanctity; and the more the population increases, the more people will respond, Amen.

After Moshe bestowed his blessing, Hashem showed him the Land of Israel. Then he died, and Hashem buried him.

Says the Gemara:[2] The Torah begins with kindness, as it is

---

1. Devarim 33:1.
2. *Sotah* 14a.

written, "Hashem, God, made Adam and his wife garments of skin, and He clothed them."[3] And it ends with kindness, as it is written, "He buried him in the valley."[4]

But Hashem's kindness began even before he clothed man — with the creation of man. Or for that matter, His kindness began with the creation of the universe, which was all for the sake of man. And certainly Hashem did a great deal of kindness for Moshe throughout his lifetime. Why, then, were these examples chosen?

Possibly, clothing them was chosen as the first example because it involves the mitzvah of *tzeniut*.[5] *Tzeniut* safeguards the holiness of the eyes and minds of the Jewish people, besides differentiating men from animals, which is certainly true. But in addition, the modest garb that Jewish women are commanded to wear contains tremendous kindness for both women and men here in this world, as anyone who thinks about it will realize.

The second example involves the mitzvah of burial. The Gemara[6] states that burial spares the dead disgrace and provides them atonement, which is certainly true. But in addition, burying the dead contains tremendous kindness for the living. It protects the mourners from grieving excessively and from despising life.

When the Gemara tells us that Torah begins and ends with kindness, it means that the entire Torah is kindness and not only will we be rewarded for keeping the Torah's mitzvot with the ultimate bliss of the world to come, but even in this world, the mitzvot give us a sweet, beautiful life.

For instance, the Ramban[7] says that eating kosher protects the

---

3. Bereshit 3:21.
4. Devarim 34:6.
5. Modesty.
6. *Sanhedrin* 46b.
7. Vayikra 11:13.

Jewish body and soul. Family purity enhances marriage. The Hinuch says that the festivals were given for rejoicing, for people need joy. Other mitzvot lead to remembering Hashem's many kindnesses and trusting in Him.

In summary, the Torah begins and ends with kindness. In fact, it is all kindness, for it gives us a sweet, beautiful life in this world and ultimate bliss in the next.